Paths to the Ancient Past

PATHS
TO THE
ANCIENT
PAST

*Applications of the Historical
Method to Ancient History*

by TOM B. JONES

Professor of Ancient History, University of Minnesota

THE FREE PRESS, NEW YORK

Collier-Macmillan Limited, London

099346

Cover design/S. A. Summit, Inc.

Preface

MORE than thirty years in the classroom have persuaded me that students in introductory history courses should be exposed not only to the subject matter but also to the methodology or discipline of history. What the historian does, how he works, is worth knowing; it is one of the elements of a liberal education. Thus, an introduction to the craft of history is just as important to the student who will never take another course in history as it is to the person who may specialize in it.

There are many ways of treating history as a discipline, and what follows here is only one of them. All I can say is that I have found it useful in teaching "ancient history."

I am most grateful to the editors of *Archaeology*, the *American Journal of Philology*, *Agricultural History*, and the *Classical World* (formerly *Classical Weekly*) for permission to reprint certain articles of mine and to the editor of the *American Journal of Archaeology* for allowing me to quote from several of Carl Blegen's reports on Troy. Specific acknowledgements will be found in the citations below.

Tom B. Jones

Contents

Paths to the Ancient Past

Introduction

THE STUDY of "ancient history" is one of the oldest and most persistent of man's intellectual pursuits. In the forty centuries that have elapsed since the earliest known dynastic lists were compiled by Sumerian scribes and Egyptian priests, scarcely a generation has gone by without some new attempt to reconstruct one part or another of the story of man from his creation to the "Fall of Rome." Much of ancient history was current rather than ancient when the first historians began to record it, and today one often feels that the classical authors were more successful in dealing with their present than with their past. It is true that from annals, chronicles, and cosmogonies there was eventual progress to the formal histories of Herodotus and Thucydides; and it is also true that the objectives and research techniques of a Polybius would not fall much below the standards of our time, but the kinds of sources employed by the professionals of antiquity as well as the historical categories (political, military, institutional) in which they were interested were closely circumscribed by comparison with twentieth-century historiography. This is not a criticism of these founders of history and giants still among historians; it is merely to suggest that vast areas of what is now considered the province of the historian were left unexplored until modern times when new interests promoted the use of new kinds of sources and the development of new techniques of research.

During the last five hundred years ancient history has been studied in degrees of intensity and areas of extent far exceeding those imagined even by the best historians who lived during the classical period. Since about A.D. 1850 this intensity has deepened immeasurably, and its extent has broadened in a comparable way. With the evolution of scientific archaeology, the decipherment of ancient scripts, the study of languages raised from the dead, and the development of new techniques for evaluating the works of the ancient authors themselves, ancient history has become a field so vast that no individual now living can claim to be an authority on the subject as a whole. In fact, most "ancient historians" of the twentieth century tend to be specialists in Mesopotamian, Egyptian, or Palestinian history or the fields of fifth-century Greece, the Mycenaean Age, the Roman Republic, and the like. One can no longer be truly expert in the larger divisions of ancient history: the ancient Near East, Greece, or Rome. In many cases specialization has become extreme, and a man may be exclusively a Greek epigrapher, an expert on prehistoric Syrian pottery, a papyrologist, a palaeographer, and so on.

After four thousand years of study, and particularly after a century of frenzied research, it is not surprising to encounter among laymen and even among specialists the feeling that there is little more to be done in ancient history as a whole or that new knowledge can only be derived from the excavation of fresh archaeological sites. It cannot be denied that the potential of archaeology is vast and as yet unrealized, but archaeology affords only one of several possible avenues of approach to the still-dark reaches of the past. A new analysis of an ancient author or a rereading of a group of authors may yield a novel point of view with regard to a specific event or a whole period. Greater familiarity with an ancient language may provide further insights into a culture. There are, for example, many Sumerian, Egyptian, and Hittite texts for which we do not have at present reliable translations; and, after all these centuries, it is still possible to improve the accuracy of Old Testament translations and so learn more about the Book of Books. Additional archaeological finds are desirable, but it is well to remember that much material dug up fifty or a hundred years ago has not yet been carefully studied, and thousands of inscriptions, papyri, and even manuscripts long ago discovered have not been published. Finally, it is not impossible to devise research techniques that will squeeze new information from old sources or make completely new sources available for use.

The historian's job is to learn *what* happened in the past and to divine, if he can, *why* it happened. The beginning student, who "takes" history, will be concerned with some of these "whats" and "whys," but it is equally important that he should learn something about history as a discipline. There *is* an historical method or approach to problem solving, just as there is a scientific method or a mathematical method. These are all-powerful tools of which the educated person should be aware and which he should be able to use in his own quest for knowledge and understanding.

How does the historian recreate the past? What is the value of archaeology, and what are its limitations? What do the ancient documents have to contribute? How does one decipher an unknown script or resurrect a dead language? What problems are encountered in dealing with the literary sources?

These are some of the specific questions which the student of ancient history ought to ask, but there are also certain more general and important questions that come to mind:

How does the historian establish a fact? How does he formulate and test his hypotheses? What are his ultimate goals?

In the pages that follow, the historical method as applied in ancient history will be presented, and it is to be hoped that the student will find there the answers to some of these questions.

Archaeology

ARCHAEOLOGY is a discipline that concerns itself with the material remains of ancient or extinct cultures and civilizations. The archaeologist uncovers, discovers, or recovers the stones and bones which are the visible relics of the fourth dimension, time. From a study of weapons, tools, pottery, metalwork, architectural and sculptural remains, the life of the past may often be reconstructed.

Archaeology has its uses—and its limitations. It can tell us *how* ancient peoples lived, but not much of what they *did* or *thought*. The archaeological often supplements or illuminates the literary record. To cite an obvious example, we should know very little about the Hebrews if it were not for the Bible. The archaeological remains in Palestine, though abundant, might never lead us to the conclusion that the Hebrews became monotheists or that they differed from their neighbors in many ways. Yet, there were many passages in the Old Testament which were obscure or misunderstood before archaeological investigation in Palestine and the adjacent countries produced illustrative material that resulted in clarification.

In the last one hundred years archaeology has passed from its infancy—or, at best, adolescence—to a measure of maturity. From an activity scarcely removed from grave-robbing it has progressed to a complex research stage that demands increasing specialization of its participants. The modern archaeologist is a professional man who has spent many years as a student and many more as an apprentice in the field to acquire the experience necessary for independent excavation.

Two misconceptions about archaeology appear to be widespread. One is the romantic view, the "Magic Spades" approach. In actual fact, archaeological research can be dull and unrewarding; it is often carried out under the most difficult and unpleasant conditions. There are times when it is no fun at all.

The other misconception is that archaeology is a science. It is true that in archaeology measurements of various kinds are taken with great care, scientific methods and devices are used wherever possible, and a good archaeologist is as objective as his nature will permit, but the exactitude of the mathematical or physical sciences is rarely achieved, and frequently the archaeologist has to content himself with the crudest approximation.

There are many good and easily accessible expositions of archaeological methods and objectives which the layman can read. He can also keep in touch with current excavations through the periodicals which report such activities. Among the periodicals especially for the layman are *Archaeology, Expedition,* and *The Biblical Archaeologist.* Good articles on archaeology frequently appear in *Natural History, The Scientific American,* and *The National Geographic.*

The contributions of archaeology to the study of the past may be illustrated by two outstanding examples: the rediscovery of Assyria and the story of the excavations at Troy. In both cases the available literary sources were inadequate and did little more than hint at the importance of two subjects which have now become fields of major interest: the ancient history of Mesopotamia and Greek prehistory. Momentous as the archaeological finds proved to be, however, it is worth noting that in both instances, the fullest interpretation of the discoveries was possible only after the decipherment of forgotten scripts enabled us to read documents uncovered by archaeological excavation.

The Rediscovery of Assyria

A century and a half ago practically everything people knew about the ancient Near East was derived from purely literary sources—most of which were incomplete, unreliable, or biased. The Old Testament, although amazingly accurate in its historical sections, had the disadvantage of presenting history from a decidedly provincial point of view. It was not, and did not pretend to be, a history of the Near East but rather the story of a particular people who lived in a limited area. In addition to the Old Testament there were works in Greek and Latin which dealt only incidentally with the Near East or were based upon other works, possibly more informative, which had ceased to exist. Our great-grandfathers read Herodotus, Josephus, Diodorus, and occasionally Strabo—and considered themselves well informed.

From the Old Testament and the classical authors, people in the early nineteenth century were reasonably familiar with the names of the Medes, Persians, Egyptians, and Babylonians as well as the Assyrians. For the scholar of A.D. 1800, however, the history of the Near East, Greece, and Rome began in the eighth century B.C.—in 776 with the first Olympiad in Greece; in 753 with the founding of Rome; and about 750 in the Near East with the first important contacts between Assyria and Israel. For previous events, the Old Testament narrative was followed, with confidence by some, with uneasiness by others, because so much was left unsaid. A glance at various editions of the *Encyclopedia Britannica* (1810–1840) will suggest no knowledge or little suspicion of earlier epochs. An "ancient history" written by Sir William Drummond in 1824 devoted 296 pages to Babylonia and Assyria, but the material consisted mostly of speculation about the location of Babylon and Nineveh and a recital of various myths about the area. This latter material had been culled, of course, from the texts of the classical authors mentioned above.

The contrast between what was known in 1800 and the information at our command today is very considerable. The limits of written history have now been pushed back from the eighth century B.C. to at least the beginning of the third millennium—a thousand years earlier than the traditional date of the great flood. Peoples and individuals whose names were previously unknown have now become almost household words: the Sumerians, Hammurabi, Ikhnaton, Ashurbanipal, and many others. Yet we might be no better informed than our fore-fathers if we were still obliged to derive our information only from the same literary sources available to them. Fortunately, a little over a century ago, two new sources of information became accessible through the work of (1) pioneer archaeologists on the one hand, and (2) early philologists on the other. Instead of speculating about the location of the fabled cities of antiquity, the archaeologists went out and found them, thus bringing to light marvelous civilizations long forgotten. At the same time, philologists undertook the decipherment of ancient scripts and the reconstruction of ancient languages unread for thousands of years. In Mesopotamia the crucial years for rediscovery were the 1840's with the excavations of Layard and Botta in Assyria, and the decipher-ment of the cuneiform script by Sir Henry Rawlinson. We shall examine the work of Layard first, and the contributions of Rawlinson will be considered in a later chapter.

The archaeological recovery of the ancient Near East proceeded in a reverse direction: from the latest periods toward the earliest, from the more or less known to the unknown. Naturally, it was the remains of antiquity in Persia, Babylonia, and Assyria that first claimed attention in that part of the world. European travelers from Benjamin of Tudela in the twelfth century A.D. to Claudius J. Rich in the nineteenth had described the ancient mounds and visible ruins of Persia and Babylon. Although doubts were expressed by some, it was generally agreed that Persepolis, Nineveh, and Babylon were represented by the ruins which we now know to have marked those ancient sites. In the seventeenth and eighteenth centuries, antiquities began to be collected by the travelers and sent back to Europe. Pietro della Valle in the early seventeenth century found inscribed bricks in Babylon that he carried to Italy. Karsten Niebuhr in the eighteenth century studied the inscriptions of Persepolis and decided correctly that no less than three systems of wedge-shaped, or cuneiform, writing were represented there. Claudius J. Rich, agent for the East India Company at Baghdad from 1811 to 1821, was the first to make careful studies of the ruins of Babylon and so point the way for future excavators. His two memoirs on Babylon were widely circulated, and, even though he wasted much time hunting for the Tower of Babel, later and less gullible workers were able to use his material as a starting point.

Nevertheless, the first serious and concentrated operations began not in Babylonia but rather in Assyria with the efforts of the Frenchman, Botta, and the Englishman, Layard. Neither were scholars nor archaeologists in the modern sense, but both differed from Rich in that they dug into the ground more or less systematically instead of wandering about collecting surface finds. The new technique paid wonderful dividends, for the discoveries of Botta and Layard, particularly in sculptural and architectural remains, were spectacular to say the least.

Emile Botta, French consul at Mosul, had dug a little at Kuyunjik (Nineveh) and a great deal at Khorsabad (another Assyrian capital) in 1842–1843, but his discoveries were, for the English-speaking world, completely eclipsed by the series of excavations conducted by Sir Austen Henry Layard at Nimrud (Biblical Calah) and Nineveh beginning in 1845. Layard published popular accounts of his work. Thousands of copies were sold in England and America. He also produced several handsome folios of etchings and lithographs which illustrated his discoveries.

Archaeology in 1845 was much different than it is today. Instead of flying out to Iraq for a season of a few months, Layard had to spend many weeks making his way to the Near East by slow steamer and then on horseback for hundreds of miles to Mosul. When he arrived there, he found himself the only European in the whole area. His papers from the Turkish government in Constantinople meant little in a region where the far-away Turkish rulers were hated by the rebellious Arabs and wild Kurdish tribesmen. A lone foreigner must steer a perilous course with the local authorities: the religious head, or *cadi*, at Mosul and the village chiefs were constantly at war. But none of this perturbed the calm assurance of Layard. He had come to dig—that was the important thing. He described the beginning of his excavations at Nimrud as follows:[1]

I had slept little during the night. The hovel in which we had taken shelter, and its inmates, did not invite slumber; but such scenes and companions were not new to me; they could have been forgotten, had my brain been less excited. Hopes, long cherished, were now to be realized, or were to end in disappointment. Visions of palaces underground, of gigantic monsters, of sculptured figures, and endless

1. A. H. Layard, *Nineveh and its Remains*, 2 vols., New York 1849, I, p. 43 ff. and *passim*.

inscriptions, floated before me. After forming plan after plan for removing the earth, and extricating these treasures, I fancied myself wandering in a maze of chambers from which I could find no outlet. Then again, all was reburied, and I was standing on the grass-covered mound. Exhausted, I was at length sinking into sleep, when hearing the voice of Awad [Layard's native foreman], I rose from my carpet, and joined him outside the hovel. The day already dawned; he had returned with six Arabs, who agreed for a small sum to work under my direction.

Fig. 1. The Mound at Nimrud. (Layard, *Monuments of Nineveh*, London 1853.)

The lofty cone and broad mound of Nimroud broke like a distant mountain on the morning sky . . . Twenty minutes' walk brought us to the principal mound. The absence of all vegetation enabled me to examine the remains with which it was covered. Broken pottery and fragments of bricks, both inscribed with the cuneiform character, were strewed on all sides. The Arabs watched my motions as I wandered to and fro, and observed with surprise the objects I had collected. They joined, however, in the search, and brought me handfuls of rubbish, amongst which I found with joy the fragment of a bas-relief. Convinced from this discovery that sculptured remains must still exist in some part of the mound . . . I dug immediately into the side, which was here very steep, and thus avoided the necessity of removing much earth. We came almost immediately to a wall, bearing inscriptions in the same character as those already described....

On the next day as they excavated a room built of stone slabs about eight feet high near the bottom of this chamber:

I found several ivory ornaments, upon which were traces of gilding; amongst them was the figure of a man in long robes . . . Awad, who had his own suspicions of the object of my search, which he could scarcely persuade himself was limited to mere stones, carefully collected all the scattered fragments of gold leaf he could find in the rubbish; and, calling me aside in a mysterious and confidential fashion, produced them wrapped up in a piece of dingy paper. "O Bey," said he, "Wallah! your books are right, and the Franks know that which is hid from the true believer. Here is the gold sure enough, and, please God, we shall find it all in a few days. Only don't say any thing about it to those Arabs, for they are asses and cannot hold their tongues. The matter will come to the ears of the Pasha." He was much surprised, and equally disappointed, when I generously presented him with the treasures he had collected, and all such as he might hereafter discover. He left me, muttering *"Yia Rubbi!"* and other pious ejaculations, and lost in conjectures as to the meanings of these strange proceedings.

As he dug around the edges of the mound, Layard found many architectural members nearly all of which were badly burned, so:

As there was a ravine running far into the mound, apparently formed by the winter rains, I determined to open a trench in the center of it [in the hope of finding ruins better preserved]. In two days the workmen reached the top of a slab, which appeared to be both well preserved, and to be still standing in its original position. On the south side I discovered, to my great satisfaction, two human figures, considerably above natural size, sculptured in low relief, and still exhibiting the freshness of a recent work. In a few hours the earth and rubbish had been completely removed from the face of the slab, no part of which had been injured. The ornaments were delicately graven on the robes, the tassels and fringes, the bracelets and armlets, the elaborate curls of the hair and beard, were all entire. The figures were back to back, and furnished with wings . . . An inscription ran across the sculpture. To the west of this slab was a cornerstone . . . which led me to a figure of singular form. A human body, clothed in robes similar to those of the winged men on the previous slab, was surmounted by the head of an eagle or of a vulture . . . On all these figures paint could be faintly distinguished.

On the morning following these discoveries, I . . . was returning to the mound, when I saw two Arabs . . . urging their mares to the top of their speed. On approaching me they stopped. "Hasten, O Bey," exclaimed one of them—"hasten to the diggers, for they have found Nimrod himself. Wallah, it is wonderful, but it is true! We have seen him with our own eyes. There is no God but God;" and both joining in this pious exclamation, they galloped off. . . .

On reaching the ruins I descended into the new trench, and found the workmen, who had already seen me, as I approached, standing near a heap of baskets and cloaks. Whilst Awad advanced, and asked for a present to celebrate the occasion, the Arabs withdrew the screen they had hastily constructed, and disclosed an enormous human head sculptured in full out of the alabaster of the country. They had uncovered the upper part of the figure, the remainder of which was still buried in the earth. I saw at once that the head must belong to a winged bull or lion, similar to those of Khorsabad and Persepolis.

This magnificent find proved a mixed blessing. Some of the workmen were terrified and ran away. People streamed out from the town to view the spectacle, and religious difficulties arose:

As I had expected, the report of the discovery of the gigantic head, carried by a terrified Arab to Mosul, had thrown the town into commotion. He had scarcely checked his speed before reaching the bridge. Entering breathless into the bazaars, he announced to everyone he met that Nimrod had appeared.

The religious authorities went into consultation, and:

Their deliberations ended in a procession to the governor, and a formal protest, on the part of the Musulmans of the town, against proceedings so directly contrary to the laws of the Koran. The Cadi had no distinct idea whether the bones of the mighty hunter had been uncovered, or only his image; nor did Ismail Pasha [the governor] very clearly remember whether Nimrod was a true-believing prophet, or an infidel. I consequently received a somewhat unintelligible message from his Excellency, to the effect that the remains should be treated with respect, and be by no means further disturbed, and that he wished the excavations to be stopped at once. . . .

After this, work lagged for some time until permission to resume the excavations could be secured from Constantinople. Eventually, too, the British Museum undertook financial sponsorship for excavations in Assyria under Layard's direction, and the digging was started again under more favorable auspices.

Fig. 2. An Assyrian Colossus. (Layard, *Monuments of Nineveh,* London 1853.)

As the excavations progressed, the splendour of Assyrian civilization began to dawn upon Layard. Here was sculpture that rivalled the achievements of Egypt and Greece. Here were vast palaces with great courtyards and myriad rooms. The walls were decorated with exciting relief sculpture that showed kings and nobles in religious and court ceremonial, victorious in battle over many nations, and devoted to the hunting of fierce animals. The scenes represented on the walls were accompanied by explanatory cuneiform texts which could not at this time be read. The famous Black Obelisk found at the close of the Nimrud excavations would have created even more of a sensation if it had been possible to read its text:

Standing at the edge of a hitherto unprofitable trench, I doubted whether I should carry it any further; but made up my mind at last, not to abandon it until my return, which would be on the following day. I mounted my horse; but had scarcely left the mound when a corner of black marble was uncovered, lying on the very edge of the trench ... An Arab was sent after me without delay, to announce the discovery, and on my return I found an obelisk completely exposed to view. I descended eagerly into the trench, and was immediately struck by the singular appearance, and evident antiquity, of the remarkable monument before me ... Although its shape was that of an obelisk, yet it was flat at the top and cut into three gradines. It was sculptured on the four sides; there were in all twenty small bas-reliefs, and above, below, and between them was carved an inscription 210 lines in length. The whole was in the best preservation ... The king is twice represented, followed by his attendants; a prisoner is at his feet, and his vizier and eunuchs are introducing men leading various animals, and carrying vases and other objects of tribute on their shoulders, or in their hands. The animals are the elephant, the rhinoceros, the Bactrian, or two-humped camel, the wild bull, the lion, a stag, and various kinds of monkeys ... The name of the king, whose deeds it appears to record, is the same as that on the centre bulls; and it is introduced by a genealogical list containing many other royal names.

The king represented on the Black Obelisk was later discovered to be Shalmaneser III, a ninth-century ruler, and one of the sculptured panels, as its accompanying inscription revealed, portrayed the Israelite king, Jehu, presenting his tribute to Shalmaneser.

Nimrud was one of the early Assyrian capitals. Its Assyrian name was Kalakh, called Calah in the Old Testament. Most of the finds made by

Layard were of the time of Ashurnazirpal, a great Assyrian king of the ninth century B.C. and the father of Shalmaneser.

After Nimrud, Layard moved to Kuyunjik, ancient Nineveh, the late Assyrian capital, where he was to excavate for many years under the auspices of the British Museum. By this time, the late 1840's and early 1850's, the decipherment of the cuneiform had been partially achieved, and a few texts could be read with some assurance. The known was gradually linked to the partially known. When Layard at Nineveh found the reliefs of Sennacherib which portrayed the capture of Lachish, everyone recalled the passages in Second Kings and Isaiah which described these events:

> Now in the fourteenth year of King Hezekiah did Sennacherib, King of Assyria, come up against all the fenced cities of Judah and took them. And Hezekiah, King of Judah, sent to the King of Assyria to Lachish saying, "I have offended . . ." (II Kings, 18).

The text accompanying the Assyrian relief reads:

> Sennacherib, king of the multitudes, King of Assyria, sat upon a house chair while the booty of Lachish passed before him.

Layard was also to make other discoveries, the importance of which were not immediately appreciated. At Nineveh in 1850 he came upon two small rooms which he described as follows:

> I shall call these chambers "the chambers of records" for, like "the house of rolls," or records, which Darius ordered to be searched for the decree of Cyrus concerning the building of the temple of Jerusalem (Ezra VI, 1) they appear to have contained the decrees of the Assyrian kings, as well as the archives of the empire. I have mentioned elsewhere that the historical records and public documents of the Assyrians were kept on tablets and cylinders of baked clay. Many specimens have been brought to this country. The importance of such relics will be readily understood. They present in a small compass an abridgement, or recapitulation, of the inscriptions on the great monuments and palace walls, giving in a chronological series the events of each monarch's reign. The writing is so minute, and the letters are so close to one another, that it requires considerable experience to separate and transcribe them. The chambers I am describing appear

to have been a depository in the palace of Nineveh for such documents. To the height of a foot or more from the floor they were
entirely filled with them; some entire, but the greater part broken
into many fragments . . . They were of different sizes; the largest
tablets were flat, and measured about nine inches by six and a half
inches; the smaller were slightly convex, and some were not more
than an inch long, with but one or two lines of writing. The cuneiform
characters on most of them were singularly sharp and well-defined,
but so minute in some instances as to be almost illegible without a
magnifying glass. These documents appear to be of various kinds.
Many are historical records . . . some seem to be royal decrees and
are stamped with the name of a king, the son of Esarhaddon; others
again are divided into parallel columns by horizontal lines, contain
lists of the gods, and probably a register of offerings made in their
temples . . . Many are sealed with seals and may prove to be legal
contracts . . . We cannot overestimate their value. They furnish us
with the materials for the complete decipherment of the cuneiform
character, for restoring the history and language of Assyria, and for
inquiring into the customs, sciences, and we may perhaps even add,
the literature of its people.

What Layard had found was the great library of Ashurbanipal, the
last major ruler of the Assyrian Empire. This Ashurbanipal was that
same king, the son of Esarhaddon, whose name was then unknown.
Here in the library were indeed the business records and the official
correspondence of the Assyrian kings from Sargon to Ashurbanipal,
documents which ran into the thousands. Even more important were
the literary remains, as Layard had shrewdly guessed, but neither he
nor anyone else then realized what the content of this literature was to
be and how it would open new vistas into the past. It was another
generation before many of the tablets were read. Among them George
Smith was to come upon the Mesopotamian story of the flood, myths of
the creation, the great Epic of Gilgamesh, and many fine hymns and
psalms reminiscent of the style of the Old Testament. Here, too, were
texts on chemistry, medicine, astronomy, and mathematics, texts of
such difficulty that it has been only within our time that translation has
been possible. In Ashurbanipal's library also were copies of texts a
thousand to fifteen hundred years older than the Assyrian documents.

Some had been translated into Assyrian; others remained in the original Old Babylonian, a Semitic language related to Assyrian; and still others were in Sumerian, a still more ancient and entirely different tongue. Not only were the texts stored in the library, but also there were dictionaries and grammars and sign lists for reading Sumerian. Without such aids, we might not be able to read the Sumerian today; as it was, a half-century and more elapsed before any facility in handling this extinct language was achieved by modern scholars.

In 1856 Layard summed up the work of the preceding decade:[2]

Although ten years have barely elapsed since the first discovery of ruins on the site of the great city of Nineveh, a mass of information, scarcely to be overrated for its importance and interest, has already been added to our previous knowledge of the early history and comparative geography of the East. When in 1849 I published the narrative of my first researches in Assyria, the numerous inscriptions recovered from the remains of the buried palaces were still almost a sealed book . . . I, then, however, expressed my belief that ere long their contents would be known with almost certainty, and that they would be found to furnish a history previously almost unknown, of one of the earliest and most powerful empires of the ancient world. Since that time the labors of English scholars and other eminent investigators on the continent have nearly led to the fulfillment of those expectations.

The story of these accomplishments will be told later, but for the present we may consider the immediate consequences of Layard's own work.

Much of what Layard did was superficial, incomplete, and many of his conclusions were faulty—but all that is unimportant. His great and permanent contributions were, after all, his rediscovery of the Assyrians and the interest which he stimulated in the ancient Near East. People were tremendously excited by the reports of Layard's work, and there was an insistence that further excavations should be made, not only in Assyria, but also in Babylonia and the Holy Land.

It was soon clear that the finds of Layard and Botta in Assyria had not disclosed the center and place of origin of Mesopotamian civilization, but that Assyrian civilization was a rather late derivative of

2. A. H. Layard, *Nineveh and Babylon*, New York 1856, p. 286 ff.

Babylonian. This encouraged digging in the lower Tigris-Euphrates valley as Layard and Botta·had dug in Assyria. Excavations were begun at Babylon and soon followed by digging at other sites.

Even to the casual observer, it was obvious that the Babylonian plain had once been dotted with great cities as large or perhaps larger than Babylon. On all sides could be seen great mounds rising from the level plain; and each one of these represented an ancient site. From the mid-1850's onward, Englishmen, Frenchmen, Germans, and Americans began to dig in these mounds: the British at the mound called Muqayyar in the far south which proved to be the ancient town of Ur; the Germans at Warka (ancient Erech); the French at Telloh (Lagash); and the Americans after 1888 at Niffer (Nippur).

It was apparent that many of these sites in the lower valley had known centuries of occupation. In the upper levels of a mound one might encounter remains of the Persian period (539–330 B.C.), then just below this the so-called Neo-Babylonian age of Nabopolassar, Nebuchadnezzar, and Nabonidus (625–539 B.C.), below that the remnants of a period contemporary with the Assyrian Empire, and so on down into the depths and into the past to the more ancient glories of Babylonia in the time of Abraham when Hammurabi ruled the land and promulgated the great code of laws which de Morgan was to find at Susa in 1901.

Yet this was not the beginning. Under the levels of the Hammurabi period of the eighteenth century B.C. were found still earlier strata which gave evidence of a brilliant civilization, that of the Sumerians, the parent of all others in the Mesopotamian area. This civilization had been in existence for more than a thousand years before Hammurabi; it was even older than the Egyptian and possessed a great art and a rich literature. Here was a civilization that had passed so completely from the memory of man that the writers of the Old Testament and of the classical period had had no knowledge of it.

In the popular mind, the twentieth-century excavations of Sir Leonard Woolley at Ur typify the process by which Sumerian civilization was rediscovered. These results were certainly brilliant and crowned with immediate success, but the story told so well by Woolley himself will not be repeated here.[3] Instead, we shall take as our example the American excavations at Nippur which began less auspiciously but which have turned out very well.

3. C. L. Woolley, *Excavations at Ur*, London 1954.

The Americans at Nippur

One of the important sites in southern Mesopotamia is Nuffar, or Niffer, the ancient Nippur. This "cathedral city," the religious center of Sumerian times, constitutes the principal site of its kind to be excavated under American auspices. Its archaeological remains are of great interest, but even more important are the Sumerian literary materials uncovered at this place.

The work at Nippur began with a series of campaigns (1888–1900) which seemed plagued by ill luck, but the new series begun in 1948 has gone very well despite disturbances in Iraq.

The story of the early excavations will be presented in the words of the Assyriologist, H. V. Hilprecht, though the reader should be forewarned that Hilprecht's remarks are always colored by his favorable opinion of himself and his rather dim view of the capabilities of his coworkers.[4]

The importance of the study of the Semitic languages and literature was early recognized in the United States. Hebrew, as the language of the Old Testament, stood naturally in the centre of general interest, as everywhere in Europe; and the numerous theological seminaries of the country and those colleges which maintained close vital relations with them were its first and principal nurseries. But in the course of time a gradual though very visible change took place with regard to the position of the Semitic languages in the curriculum of all the prominent American colleges. The German idea of a university gained ground in the new world, finding its enthusiastic advocates among the hundreds and thousands of students who had come into personal contact with the great scientific leaders in Europe, and who for a while had felt the powerful spell of the new life which emanated from the class rooms and seminaries of the German universities. Post-graduate departments were organized, independent chairs of Semitic languages were established, and even archaeological museums were founded and maintained by private contributions. Salaries in some cases could not be given to the pioneers in this new movement. They stood up for a cause in which they

4. H. V. Hilprecht, *The Excavations in Assyria and Babylonia*, Philadelphia 1904, pp. 289 ff.

themselves fully believed, but the value of which had to be demonstrated. . . .

The study of the cuneiform languages, especially of Assyrian, rapidly became popular at the American universities. The romantic story of the discovery and excavation of Nineveh so graphically told by Layard, and the immediate bearing of his magnificent results upon the interpretation of the Old Testament and upon the history of art and human civilization in general, appealed at once to the religious sentiment and general intelligence of the people. The American Oriental Society and the Society of Biblical Literature and Exegesis became the first scientific exponents of the growing interest in the lands of Ashurbanipal and Nebuchadnezzar. . . .

Under the auspices of the American Oriental Society an exploratory expedition was made to Babylonia—the so-called Wolfe Expedition—in 1884, but this was merely a survey lasting a few weeks, and no digging was done. Then, in 1886, after the Rev. J. P. Peters had been appointed Professor of Hebrew at the University of Pennsylvania and the German Assyriologist, H. V. Hilprecht, had also arrived there, more serious preparations were begun for an American excavation in Babylonia. A Babylonian Exploration Fund was established in 1887; Nippur was selected as the site to be dug; and four campaigns were conducted between 1888–1900.

The staff of the first campaign consisted of Peters as director; R. F. Harper, a young Assyriologist from Yale who was later to edit the Code of Hammurabi; J. D. Prince of Columbia, who subsequently became a prominent American Sumerologist; P. H. Field, architect and surveyor; and two members of the Wolfe Expedition: J. H. Haynes, photographer, and D. Z. Noorian, interpreter. Hilprecht was added to the staff before it set out for Nippur. Prince, "having fallen seriously ill on the way down the Euphrates Valley, left the expedition at Baghdad, and returned to America by way of India and China." At last, the travelers arrived at Nippur in the midst of an Arab tribal war.

The extent of the site was impressive:

Even at a distance I began to realize that not twenty, not fifty years would suffice to excavate this important site thoroughly. What would our committee at home have said at the sight of this enormous ruin, resembling more a picturesque mountain range than the last impressive remains of human constructions! . . . But there was not much time for these and similar reflections . . . The whole neighborhood was inflamed by war. Gesticulating groups of armed men watched our approach with fear and suspicion . . . Immediately after our arrival we began to pitch our tents on the highest point of the southwestern half of the ruins, where we could enjoy an unlimited view of the swamps and the desert, and which at the same time seemed best protected against malaria and possible attacks from the Arabs.

After some desultory digging, "Tablet Hill" was discovered in the northeast half of the ruins. In a few weeks, more than two thousand cuneiform documents had been unearthed. Though many eras were represented in these finds, the majority were of the Old Babylonian period.

They consisted of business documents . . . and of tablets of a decided literary character, comprising some very fine syllabaries and lists of synonyms, letters, mathematical, astronomical, medical and religious texts, besides a few specimens of drawing and a considerable number of mostly round tablets which must be classified as school exercises . . . about fourth-fifths of the tablets were literary. . . .

Soon after we had reached Nuffar, Dr. Peters had made us acquainted with the low ebb in the finances of the expedition. It was, therefore, decided to close the excavations of the first campaign at the beginning of May [1889]. But the working season was brought to a conclusion more quickly than could have been anticipated. The trouble started with the Arabs . . . Two of the principal tribes, the Hamza and the Behatha, both of which laid claim to the mounds we had occupied and insisted on furnishing the workmen for our excavations, were at war with each other. At the slightest provocation and frequently without any apparent reason they threw their scrapers and baskets away and commenced the war-dance, brandishing their spears or guns in the air and chanting some defiant sentence especially made up for the occasion, as . . . "The last day has come," "Down with the Christians," "Matches in his beard who contradicts us," etc. The Turkish commissioner and the soldiers . . . picked frequent quarrels with the natives and irritated them with their overbearing manners. The Arabs, on the other hand, were not slow in showing their absolute independence by wandering unmolested around the camp, entering our private tents and examining our goods, like a crowd of naughty boys; or by squatting with their guns and clubs near the trenches and hurling taunting and offensive expressions at the Ottoman government.

It was also a mistake that we had pitched our tents at the top of the ruins. For as the mounds of Nuffar had no recognized owner . . . we were practically under nobody's protection, while by our conspicuous position we not only suffered from hot winds and suffocating sand storms, but invited plundering by any loiterer and marauder in the neighborhood . . . What wonder that the simple-minded children of the desert and the half-naked peasants of the marshes, who noticed our strange mode of living and saw so many unknown things for which they had no need themselves, shook their heads in amazement. On the one hand they observed how we spent large sums of money for uncovering old walls and gathering broken pottery, and on the other they found us eating the wild boar of the jungles, ignoring Arab etiquette, and violating the sacred and universal law of hospitality in the most flagrant way . . . reasons enough to regard us either as pitiable idiots whom they could easily fleece or as unclean and uncouth barbarians to whom a pious Shiite was infinitely superior.

There were threats to burn out the foreigners; there was vandalism and thievery. Then a marauder was shot in the night. All offers of indemnity were refused, and the camp was put under siege.

The whole expedition was in readiness to vacate the mounds and to force their way to Hillah, when . . . an Arab secretly set fire to our huts of reeds and mats and laid the whole camp in ashes in the short space of five minutes. For a while the utmost confusion prevailed, the soldiers got demoralized, and occupied a neighboring hill; and while we were trying to save our effects, many of the Arabs commenced plundering. Half the horses perished in the flames, firearms and saddlebags and $1000 in gold fell into the hands of the marauders, but all the antiquities were saved. Under the war-dance and yells of the frantic Arabs the expedition finally withdrew in two divisions. . . .

On the way to Baghdad Harper handed in his resignation, Field gave his own a day later, Haynes, who had been appointed United States Consul at Baghdad, prepared to remain . . . with Noorian to await further developments, Peters was recalled by cable to America. . . .

In 1890, a second expedition headed by Peters and Haynes returned to Nippur. There had been a cholera epidemic which had had a chastening effect upon the natives, and Peters took advantage of their mood:

The notion was spread among the . . . tribes that the foreigners were armed with great magical power, and that, in punishment of the firing and plundering of their camp, they had brought upon their enemies the cholera, which was not quite extinct even in the year following. Several successful treatments of light ailments, and exceedingly bitter concoctions wisely administered to various healthy chiefs, served only to assure and confirm this belief; and Peters, on his part, seized every opportunity to encourage and to develop such sentiment . . . He intimated that nothing was hidden from his knowledge, and that the accursed money which had been stolen would find its way back to him; he made mysterious threats of sore affliction and loss by death which would cause consternation among them; and to demonstrate his superior power and to indicate some of the terrible things which might happen at any moment, he finally gave them a drastic exhibition of his cunning art, which had a tremendous effect upon all who saw it. We will quote the story in his own language:

"Just before sunset, when the men were all in camp and at leisure, so that I was sure they would notice what we did, Noorian and I ascended a high point of the mound nearby, he solemnly bearing a compass before me on an improvised black cushion. There, by the side of an old trench, we went through a complicated hocus-pocus with the compass, a Turkish dictionary, a spring tape-measure, and a pair of field glasses, the whole camp watching us in puzzled wonder. Immediately after our dinner, while most of the men were still busy eating, we stole up the hill, having left to Haynes the duty of preventing any one from leaving the camp. Our fireworks were somewhat primitive and slightly dangerous, so that the trench which we had chosen for our operations proved rather close quarters. The first rocket had scarcely gone off when we could hear a buzz of excited voices below us. When the second and third followed, the cry arose that we were making the stars fall from heaven. The women screamed and hid themselves in the huts, and the more timid among the men followed suit. As Roman candles and Bengal lights followed, the excitement grew more intense. At last we came to our *pièce de résistance*, the tomato-can firework. Then, at first this fizzled and bade fair to ruin our whole performance, but just as we despaired of success, it exploded with a great noise, knocking us over backward in the trench, behind a wall in which we were hidden, and filling the air with fiery serpents hissing and sputtering in every direction. The effect was indescribably diabolical, and every man, woman, and child, guards included, fled screaming, to seek for hiding places, overcome with terror."

Archaeologically, the second expedition was not such an outstanding success. The work of the first season was continued, and about 8000 new tablets were found. A third campaign, conducted virtually single-handed by Haynes from 1893–1896, uncovered more of the site and resulted in the discovery of 21,000 cuneiform inscriptions, and in a final campaign (1898–1900) Hilprecht and Haynes were able to clarify somewhat the stratification of the site and to locate several important structures of various periods: a Parthian palace, the temple library on Tablet Hill, and the great temple of Enlil, the E-kur.

In the last analysis, however, it was the cuneiform documents that were of the greatest importance. The great number of Old Babylonian contracts, the documents of the Kassite period, the abundant Neo-Babylonian contracts (including the business records of the fifth-century B.C. "firm of Murashu and Sons"), a cuneiform map of Nippur with the principal buildings clearly identified, and many dedicatory inscriptions of all periods provided a rich harvest. But all this paled into insignificance beside the finds of literary texts, mostly in Sumerian, which had been kept in the temple school and library. Hymns, psalms, epics—the Sumerian version of the flood story, and the ballads of the Gilgamesh cycle—as well as Old Babylonian mathematical and astronomical texts.

The full significance of the literary finds has only been recognized during the last generation when it has been possible to read Sumerian with some facility. Largely through the work of Prof. S. N. Kramer and his students the epics, proverbs, fables, and other literary types have been identified and published just as Prof. Otto Neugebauer and others have clarified the mathematical and astronomical texts. Parenthetically, it was not merely the difficulties presented by the Sumerian language that impeded progress, but also the fact that the finds from Nippur were divided between the Ottoman government and the University of

Pennsylvania. The result was that the tablets were divided on a numerical basis: one fragment in this basket, and one fragment in that. Consequently, certain portions of a single tablet which had been broken might end up in Istanbul and others in Philadelphia, and this complicated the process of reassembling the text considerably.

The supply of tablets from the early series at Nippur had by no means been exhausted when excavations were resumed in 1948 under the auspices of the University Museum of the University of Pennsylvania and the Oriental Institute of the University of Chicago. Nevertheless, since other sites had yielded only about one fifth of the total volume of known literary texts compared with the four fifths provided by Nippur alone, it seemed essential to return to Nippur. In the years that followed, thousands of new tablets were found in the scribal quarter, but also more mature archaeological techniques have led to the discovery, identification, and study of new areas and structures on the site.

The Excavation of Troy

As a further illustration of what archaeology has contributed to the study of the past and also to demonstrate how archaeology has matured since the middle of the last century, we may now turn to the story of the excavations at Troy.

Our great-grandfathers were divided in their opinions about the legend of Troy and the Trojan War. Had Homer chosen an historical background for the *Iliad*? Or was it all pure fiction? Had Troy ever existed? Had people once lived in the manner described by Homer?

The Greeks and Romans for the most part had accepted the Trojan War as historical fact and had agreed to date it about 1200 B.C., but, for many people living a century ago, it seemed unlikely that any Greek history prior to the date of the First Olympiad (776 B.C.) would ever be known. In 1829, Goldsmith pronounced:

> The first notices we have of every country are fabulous and uncertain. Among an unenlightened people every imposture is likely

to take place, for ignorance is the parent of credulity. Nothing, therefore, which the Greeks have transmitted to us concerning their earliest state can be relied on. The fabulous age, therefore, of Greece must have no place in history.

Here was a matter that could be resolved only by finding—or not finding—Troy. Heinrich Schliemann (1822–1890), whose own story will be presented here, identified Troy to his own satisfaction, although even after he had dug there for twenty years there were still skeptics who insisted that he had not found Troy. One man even denied that Schliemann's site had been occupied by a town; he argued that it was a hill which had been used as a fire altar.

The digging at Troy did not end with Schliemann. New finds and new interpretations were made later by Wilhelm Dörpfeld and Carl Blegen, as we shall see. What Schliemann did, however, was extremely important: he restored men's faith in the existence of the Greek Heroic (Mycenaean) Age and aroused the interest and activity that has led to our present knowledge of that remote period, an age which, now that its inscriptions can be read, can no longer be called prehistoric.

This is Schliemann's own account:[5]

If I begin this book with my autobiography, it is not from any feeling of vanity, but from a desire to show how the work of my later life has been the natural consequence of the impressions I received in my earliest childhood; and that, so to say, the pickaxe and spade for the excavation of Troy and the royal tombs of Mycenae were both forged and sharpened in the little German village in which I passed eight years of my earliest childhood. I also find it necessary to relate how I obtained the means which enabled me, in the autumn of my life, to realize the great projects I formed when I was a poor little boy. But I flatter myself that the manner in which I have employed my time, as well as the use I have made of my wealth, will meet with general approbation, and that my autobiography may aid in diffusing among the intelligent public of all countries a taste for those high and noble studies, which have sustained my courage during the hard trials of my life, and which will sweeten the days yet left me to live.

I was born on the 6th of January, 1822, in the little town of Neu

5. H. Schliemann, *Troy and its Remains*, New York 1874, p. 1 and *passim*.

Buckow, in Mecklenburg-Schwerin, where my father, Ernest Schliemann, was a Protestant clergyman . . . Though my father was neither a scholar nor an archaeologist, he had a passion for ancient history. He often told me with warm enthusiasm of the tragic fate of Herculaneum and Pompeii, and seemed to consider him the luckiest of men who had the means and the time to visit the excavations which were going on there. He also related to me with admiration the great deeds of the Homeric heroes and the events of the Trojan War, always finding in me a warm defender of the Trojan cause. With great grief I heard from him that Troy had been so completely destroyed, that it had disappeared without leaving any traces of its existence. My joy may be imagined, therefore, when, being nearly eight years old, I received from him, in 1829, as a Christmas gift, Dr. Georg Ludwig Jerrer's *Universal History*, with an engraving representing Troy in flames, with its huge walls and the Scaean gate, from which Aeneas is escaping, carrying his father Anchises on his back and holding his son Ascanius by the hand; and I cried out, "Father, you were mistaken: Jerrer must have seen Troy, otherwise he could not have represented it here." "My son," he replied, "that is merely a fanciful picture." But to my question whether ancient Troy had such huge walls as those depicted in the book, he answered in the affirmative. "Father," retorted I, "if such walls once existed, they cannot possibly have been completely destroyed: vast ruins of them must still remain, but they are hidden away beneath the dust of ages." He maintained the contrary, whilst I remained firm in my opinion, and at last we both agreed that I should one day excavate Troy.

What weighs in our heart, be it joy or sorrow, always finds utterance from our lips, especially in childhood; and so it happened that I talked of nothing else to my playfellows, but of Troy. . . Thanks to God, my firm belief in the existence of that Troy has never forsaken me amid the vicissitudes of my eventful career; but it was not destined for me to realize till in the autumn of my life . . . sweet dreams of fifty years ago.

The next few years were not happy ones for Schliemann: the death of his mother when he was only nine; the disruption of the family; the movement of his father from one parish to another; and the termination of his formal education in 1836 when, at fourteen, he was apprenticed to a grocer in Fürstenberg.

> I was employed in the little grocer's shop . . . for five years and a half . . . My occupation consisted in retailing herrings, butter, potato-whiskey, milk, salt, coffee, sugar, oil, and candles; in grinding potatoes for the still, sweeping the shop, and the like employments. Our transactions were on such a small scale, that our aggregate sales hardly amounted to 3000 thalers . . . annually; nay, we thought we had extraordinary luck when we sold two pounds' worth of groceries in a day. There I of course came in contact only with the lowest classes of society. I was engaged from five in the morning till eleven at night, and had not a moment's leisure for study. Moreover I rapidly forgot the little that I had learnt in childhood; but I did not lose the love of learning; indeed I never lost it, and, as long as I live, I shall never forget the evening when a drunken miller came into the shop. His name was Hermann Niederhöffer. He was the son of a Protestant clergyman in Roebel (Mecklenberg), and had almost completed his studies at the Gymnasium of Neu Ruppin, when he was expelled on account of his bad conduct. Not knowing what to do with him, his father had apprenticed him for two years to the miller Dettmann at Güstrow. Dissatisfied with his lot, the young man gave himself up to drink, which, however, had not made him forget his Homer; for on the evening that he entered the shop he recited to us about a hundred lines of the poet, observing the rhythmic cadence of the verses. Although I did not understand a syllable, the melodious sound of the words made a deep impression on me, and I wept bitter tears over my unhappy fate. Three times over did I get him to repeat to me those divine verses, rewarding his trouble with three glasses of whiskey, which I bought with the few pence that made up my whole fortune. From that moment I never ceased to pray God that by his grace I might yet have the happiness of learning Greek.

Schliemann left the store after an injury made it impossible for him to perform heavy work. When he failed to find suitable employment in Hamburg, he determined to try his luck in South America. In 1841, he set sail for Venezuela, but his ship sank in a storm just after leaving port. Then . . .

> I intended to proceed to Amsterdam to enlist as a soldier, for I was

utterly destitute, and saw, for the moment, no other means of earning a living . . . Fortune did not smile on me at first in Amsterdam: winter had set in; I had no coat, and was suffering cruelly from the cold. My intention to enlist as a soldier could not be realized so soon as I had imagined . . . As my means of living were entirely exhausted, I feigned illness and was taken into the hospital. . . .

Early in 1842, however, Schliemann became a clerk in an import-export establishment at Amsterdam.

In my new situation my work consisted in stamping bills of exchange and getting them cashed in the town, and in carrying letters to and from the post-office. This mechanical occupation suited me, for it left me time to think of my neglected education.

First of all I took pains to learn to write legibly, and this I succeeded in doing after twenty lessons from the famous calligraphist Magnée of Brussels. Afterwards, in order to improve my position, I applied myself to the study of modern languages. My annual salary amounted only to 800 francs, half of which I spent upon my studies; on the other half I lived—miserably enough, to be sure. My lodging, which cost 8 francs a month, was a wretched garret without a fire, where I shivered with cold in winter and was scorched with the heat in summer. My breakfast consisted of rye-meal porridge, and my dinner never cost more than two-pence. But nothing spurs one on to study more than misery and the certain prospect of being able to release oneself from it by unremitting work . . . I applied myself with extra-ordinary diligence to the study of English. Necessity taught me a method which greatly facilitates the study of a language. This method consists in reading a great deal aloud, without making a translation, taking a lesson every day, constantly writing essays upon subjects of interest, correcting these under the supervision of a teacher, learning them by heart, and repeating in the next lesson what was corrected on the previous day. My memory was bad, since from childhood it had not been exercised upon any object; but I made use of every moment, and even stole time for study. In order to acquire a good pronunciation quickly, I went twice every Sunday to the English church, and repeated to myself in a low voice every word of the clergyman's sermon. I never went on my errands, even in the rain without having my book in my hand and learning something by heart; and I never waited at the post-office without reading. By such methods I gradually strengthened my memory, and in three months' time found no difficulty in reciting from memory to my teacher, Mr. Taylor, in each day's lesson, word by word, twenty printed pages, after having read them over three times attentively. In this way I committed to memory the whole of Goldsmith's *Vicar of Wakefield* and Sir Walter Scott's *Ivanhoe*. From over-excitement I slept but little, and employed my sleepless hours at night in going over in my mind what I had read on the preceding evening . . . Thus I succeeded in acquiring in half a year a thorough knowledge of the English language.

I then applied the same method to the study of French, the difficulties of which I overcame likewise in another six months. Of French authors I learned by heart the whole of Fénelon's *Aventures de Télémaque* and Bernardin de Saint Pierre's *Paul et Virginie*. This unremitting study had in the course of a single year strengthened my memory to such a degree, that the study of Dutch, Spanish, Italian, and Portuguese appeared very easy, and it did not take me more than six weeks to write and speak each of these languages fluently.

Whether from my continual readings in a loud voice, or from the effect of the moist air of Holland, my complaint in the chest gradually disappeared. . . .

Schliemann's linguistic studies took some of the time which his employers thought should be devoted to his "mechanical occupation" in their office, but in 1844 he was able to find a better position as a book-keeper with a similar firm, and . . .

As I thought that I could make myself still more useful by a knowledge of Russian, I set to work to learn that language also. But the only Russian books I could procure were an old grammar, a lexicon, and a bad translation of *Les Aventures de Télémaque*. In spite of all my enquiries, I could not find a teacher of Russian . . . so I betook myself to the study of it without a master, and, with the help of the grammar, I learned the Russian letters and their pronunciation in a few days. Then, following my old method, I began to write short stories of my own composition, and to learn them by heart . . . I tried at the same time to correct my mistakes by the practical exercise of learning the Russian *Aventures de Télémaque* by heart. It occurred to

me that I should make more progress if I had some one to whom I
could relate the adventures of Telemachus; so I hired a poor Jew for
four francs a week, who had to come every evening for two hours
to listen to my Russian recitations, of which he did not understand a
syllable.

Fluency in Russian led in 1846 to Schliemann's appointment as the
representative of his firm in St. Petersburg. With a real flair for business,
good luck, and some shrewd profiteering during the Crimean War
along with speculation in cotton at the beginning of the Civil War in
the United States, Schliemann was able to retire in 1863, independently
wealthy at the age of forty-one. By this time he had also learned Swedish,
Polish, Arabic, modern Greek, and finally realized his dream of learning
the ancient language, too. After a world tour (1864–1866), he was nearly
ready to begin the search for Troy.

On the Asiatic side of the Dardanelles lay the ruins of New Ilium,
a Greco-Roman city easily identifiable through the fragments of inscriptions lying about on the site. This was the town most of the ancient
had agreed was "Troy." As such, it had enjoyed a flourishing tourist
trade in Greek and Roman times. In 1868 . . .

My particular attention was attracted to the spot by the imposing
position and natural fortifications of the hill called HISSARLIK, which
formed the northwestern corner of Novum Ilium, and seemed to me
to mark the site of its Acropolis . . . In April 1870 I was able to return
to Hissarlik and make a preliminary excavation, in order to test the
depth to which the artificial soil extended. I made it at the northwestern corner, in a place where the hill had increased considerably
in size, and where, consequently, the accumulation of debris of the
Hellenic period was very great. Hence it was only after digging 16 feet
below the surface, that I laid bare a wall of huge stones, six and a
half feet thick, which, as my later excavations have shown, belonged
to a tower of the Macedonian epoch.

In 1871 a permit to conduct a major excavation was secured from
the Turkish government.

At length, on the 27th of September, I made my way to the
Dardanelles, together with my wife, Sophia Schliemann, who is a

native of Athens and a warm admirer of Homer, and who, with glad enthusiasm, joined me in executing the great work . . . After working with an average number of eighty laborers daily [from October 11] up to the 24th of November, we were compelled to cease the excavations for the winter. But during that interval we had been able to make a large trench on the face of the steep northern slope, and to dig down to a depth of thirty-three feet below the surface of the hill.

We first found there the remains of later Aeolic Ilium, which, on an average, reached to a depth of about six and a half feet . . . Below these Hellenic ruins, and to a depth of about thirteen feet, the debris contained a few stones, and some very coarse hand-made pottery. Below this stratum I came to a large number of house walls, of unwrought stones cemented with earth, and, for the first time, met with immense quantities of stone implements and saddle-querns, together with more coarse hand-made pottery . . . At a depth of thirty feet and thirty-three feet we discovered fragments of house-walls of large stones, many of them rudely hewn; we also came upon a great many very large blocks. The stones of these house walls appeared as if they had been separated from one another by a violent earthquake. My instruments for excavating were very imperfect: I had to work with only pickaxes, wooden shovels, baskets, and eight wheelbarrows.

I returned to Hissarlik with my wife at the end of March 1872, and resumed the excavations with 100 workmen. But I was soon able to increase the number of my laborers to 130, and had often even 150 men at work. I was now well prepared for the work, having been provided with the very best English wheelbarrows, pickaxes, and spades, and having also procured three overseers and an engineer, Mr. A. Laurent, to make maps and plans. The last received monthly 20 pounds, the overseers 6 pounds each, and my servant 7 pounds, 4 shillings; whilst the daily wages of my common laborers were 1 fr. 80 c., or about 18 pence sterling. I now built on the top of Hissarlik a wooden house, with three rooms and a magazine, kitchen, etc., and covered the buildings with waterproof felt to protect them from the rain.

On the steep northern slope of Hissarlik, which rises at an angle of 45°, and at a perpendicular depth of 46½ feet below the surface, I dug out a platform 233 feet wide, and found there an immense number of poisonous snakes; among them remarkably numerous specimens of the small brown adder called *antelion*, which is hardly thicker than an earthworm, and gets its name from the vulgar belief, that the person bitten by it only survives till sunset.

I first struck the bed rock at a depth of about 53 feet below the surface of the hill, and found the lowest stratum of artificial soil to consist of very compact debris of houses . . . This lowest stratum was succeeded by house-walls built of large limestone blocks . . . There is no trace of a general conflagration, either in this stratum of buildings built with large stones or in the lowest layer of debris. As it was my object to excavate TROY, which I expected to find in one of the lower cities, I was forced to demolish many interesting ruins in the upper strata . . . each stratum represents the ruins of a distinct city . . . The debris of the lower stratum being as hard as stone . . . I found it easier to undermine it by cutting it vertically . . . but I found this manner of excavating very dangerous, two workmen having been buried alive under a mass of debris of 2560 cubic feet, and having been saved as by a miracle. In consequence of this accident I gave up the idea of running the great platform 233 feet broad through the whole length of the hill, and decided on first digging a trench, 98 feet wide at the top and 65 feet at the bottom.

This was a sound scheme: the stratification could be seen from the trench, and side trenches could be made if anything interesting was discovered. As he had announced, Schliemann was interested only in TROY. When he found one of the lower strata covered with a burned layer, he identified it as Homeric Troy. This was first called the Second City, but by 1878 he had decided that two "cities" lay below it, so the "Second City" was renamed the Third. The decisive campaign in Schliemann's discovery of "Troy" was carried out in 1873:

I ceased excavating in the 14th of August, 1872, and resumed my operations, in company with my wife, on the first of February of the following year. In the preceding autumn, by the side of my two wooden buildings, we had built a house for ourselves composed of stones brought to light in my excavations, and had made the walls two feet thick; but we were compelled to let our foremen occupy it, as they were not sufficiently provided with clothes and wrappers, and would otherwise have perished during the great cold of the winter. My poor wife and myself, therefore, suffered very much, since the icy north wind blew with such violence through the chinks of our house-walls, which were made of planks, that although we had a fire on the hearth, yet the thermometer showed −4° Réamur or 23° Fahrenheit, while the water which stood near the hearth froze into solid masses. During the day we could to some degree bear the cold by working in the excavations, but in the evenings we had nothing to keep us warm except our enthusiasm for the great work of discovering Troy.

Once we had the narrowest possible escape from being burnt alive. The stones of our fireplace rested merely upon the boards of the floor, and, whether through a crevice in the cement between the stones or from some other cause, one night the floor took fire; and when I accidentally awoke at 3 o'clock, I found flames extending over a large part of it. The room was filled with dense smoke, and the north wall was just beginning to catch fire; a few seconds would have sufficed to burn a hole into it, and the whole house would then have been in flames in less than a minute, for a high north gale was blowing on that side. I did not, however, lose my presence of mind. Pouring the contents of a bath upon the burning wall, I at once stopped the fire in that direction. Our cries awoke a labourer who was asleep in an adjoining room, and he called the foremen from the stone house to our assistance. Without losing a moment they fetched hammers, iron levers, and pickaxes; the floor was broken up, torn to pieces, and quantities of damp earth thrown upon it, as we had no water. But, as the lower beams were burning in many places, a quarter of an hour elapsed before we got the fire under and all danger was at an end.

The great cold did not last very long, and we afterwards had splendid weather . . . From about the 1st of March we heard the perpetual croaking of millions of frogs in the surrounding marshes, and in the second week of March the storks returned. One of the many discomforts of our life in the wilderness we inhabited was the hideous shrieking of innumerable owls, which built their nests in the holes of my trenches; their shrieks had a weird and terrible sound, and were especially intolerable at night.

Up to the beginning of May 1873, I had believed that the hill of Hissarlik, where I was excavating, marked the site of the Trojan citadel only; and it certainly is the fact that Hissarlik was the Acropolis of Novum Ilium. I therefore imagined that Troy was larger than the latter town, or at least as large; but I thought it important to discover the precise limits of the Homeric city, and accordingly I sank twenty shafts as far down as the rock on the west, south-west, south-south-east, and east of Hissarlik, directly at its foot or at some distance from it, on the plateau of the Ilium of Greek colony . . . It appears certain that the ancient city cannot have extended on any side beyond the primeval plateau of Hissarlik. . . .

Wishing to investigate the fortifications on the west and north-west sides of the ancient city, in the beginning of May 1873 I also commenced making a trench, 33 feet broad and 141 feet long, on the north-west side of the hill, at the very point where I had made the first trench in April 1870. I first broke through an Hellenic circuit wall, probably that which, according to Plutarch in his Life of Alexander, was built by Lysimachus . . . In order to hasten the excavations on the north-west side of the hill, I cut a deep trench from the west side also, in which, unfortunately, I struck obliquely the circuit-wall of Lysimachus, and was consequently compelled to remove a double quantity of stones to force a way through it. . . .

While following up this circuit-wall, and bringing more and more of it to light . . . I struck upon a large copper article of the most remarkable form, which attracted my attention all the more, as I thought I saw gold behind it. On the top of it was a layer of red and calcined ruins, from 4¾ to 5¼ feet thick, as hard as stone, and above this again a wall of fortification built of large stones and earth, which must have been erected shortly after the destruction of Troy. In order to secure the treasure from my workmen and save it for archaeology, it was necessary to lose no time; so, although it was not yet the hour for breakfast, I immediately had the *païdos* called. This is a word of uncertain derivation, which has passed over into Turkish, and is here employed in place of *anapausis*, or time for rest. While the men were eating and resting, I cut out the Treasure with a large knife. This required great exertion and involved great risk, since the wall of fortification, beneath which I had to dig, threatened every moment to fall down upon me. But the sight of so many objects, every one of which is of inestimable value to archaeology, made me reckless, and I never thought of any danger. It would, however, have been impossible for me to have removed the treasure without the help of my dear wife, who stood at my side, ready to pack the things I cut out in her shawl, and to carry them away.

As I found all these articles together, in the form of a rectangular mass, or packed into one another, it seems certain that they were placed on the city wall in a wooden chest. This supposition seems to me to be corroborated by the fact that close by the side of these articles I found a copper key. It is therefore possible that some one packed the treasure in the chest, and carried it off, without having had time to pull out the key; when he reached the wall, however, the hand of an enemy, or the fire overtook him, and he was obliged to abandon the chest, which was immediately covered, to a height of 5 feet, with the ashes and stones of the adjoining house.

That the treasure was packed together at a moment of extreme peril appears to be proved, among other things, by the contents of the largest silver vase, consisting of nearly 9000 objects of gold . . . Hoping to find more treasures here, I pulled down the upper wall . . . but to do this I had to pull down the larger of my wooden houses. . . .

This was the "Treasure of Priam," as Schliemann called it, and its discovery, covered as it was by a "burned layer," convinced him that he had found TROY. In his first major report, the *Troianische Alterthümer* which was published in Leipzig in 1874 and of which an English version, *Troy and its Remains*, appeared in the same year, Schliemann distinguished five, possibly six, layers of occupation at Hissarlik: the Greco-Roman city at the top, extending down $6\frac{1}{2}$ feet from the original ground level; a very shallow unidentifiable stratum just below this; the Fourth City, $6\frac{1}{2}$–13 feet below the surface; the Third City, 13–23 feet; the Second City, TROY, 23–33 feet; and the First City, 33–$46/52\frac{1}{2}$ feet.

In 1874, Schliemann began excavating in Greece at Mycenae, the legendary home of Agamemnon, leader of the Greeks in the Trojan War. Mycenae yielded spectacular finds which confirmed Schliemann's belief in the historicity of the Homeric poems and persuaded many skeptics that he was, after all, on the right track.

Further excavations were made at Troy in 1878 and 1879, and another season at Troy was initiated in 1882. In the latter year Schliemann was assisted by a brilliant young German archaeologist, Wilhelm Dörpfeld, who had been trained in the new scientific methods developed in the

German universities and who already had some field experience at Olympia, a classical site. In 1884, Schliemann and Dörpfeld also excavated in Greece at Tiryns, near Mycenae, where they found a Mycenaean palace in a much better state of preservation than the one at Mycenae.

The discoveries at Mycenae and Tiryns and the application of more rigorous methods of excavation at Troy, however, suggested certain inconsistencies in the evidence which had at first made it appear that "Troy" and Mycenae were contemporary. By comparison with Mycenae, the Second City at Troy, the one covered by the "burned layer," seemed small and primitive, hardly worth the effort to capture it which the Greek heroes were supposed to have made. Its jewelry and pottery were crude and quite unlike the handsome treasures found by Schliemann in the shaft graves at Mycenae and the sophisticated Mycenaean painted pottery of Mycenae and Tiryns. Moreover, the mainland Greek architectural styles and the types of fortification of the Mycenaean period were more advanced than those of Troy II. Another disturbing find had been made at Orchomenos in central Greece about 1880 where a distinctive kind of pottery called Minyan was found in a layer below—and therefore earlier than—a stratum containing Mycenaean pottery. At Troy, Schliemann had found this Minyan ware *in the Fifth City* which, if the Second City was Troy, must be dated later than the Mycenaean period.

Late in 1889 and during the first half of 1890, Schliemann dug for the last time at Troy. Moving out from the center of the citadel, or acropolis, to the west side of the hill which had been hitherto untouched, Schliemann and Dörpfeld made a momentous discovery, one not immediately appreciated:[6]

> Most noteworthy, on account of its buildings made of huge dressed blocks, is the fourth settlement from the top, in which has been found the curious grey or black monochrome [Minyan] pottery, which I formerly held to be Lydian. Every single house belonging to this colony within the citadel had been cleared away by the Romans, and there remained only pottery . . . Here, however, on the west side, beyond the Trojan Pergamos [the circuit walls of Troy II], but within the Roman and Greek Acropolis . . . we struck at a depth of 23 feet below the surface upon this remarkable settlement, which

6. K. Schuchhardt, *Schliemann's Excavations*, New York 1891, p. 330 ff.

itself reaches to a depth of 7 feet. Along with the monochrome pottery there appears a great deal of painted pottery belonging to what we usually regard as the most ancient Greek [Mycenaean] type. Among these we should specially note the Mycenaean cups with stirrup handles, painted with parallel bands. Their shape is that most usually found at Mycenae and Tiryns. Similar vases have also been found by Mr. Flinders Petrie at the pyramids of Ilahun . . . in graves [in Egypt] of the time of Rameses II.

So Schliemann, but Dörpfeld also reported:

The fourth layer was the most important; in it several buildings constructed of large blocks of stone were laid bare. The ground plan of one of these buildings can be tolerably well made out, although it has not yet been completely excavated; it resembles a simple Greek temple or the megaron of the royal palace [of the Mycenaean period as shown by the excavations at Mycenae and Tiryns] . . . The building is of great importance for the history of Trojan antiquities, for in it and in its debris several Mycenaean vases and fragments of vases have been found . . . This circumstance not only dates this layer approximately, but allows us to draw the further conclusion that the second stratum . . . must be older than this stratum with the Mycenaean vases.

Schliemann died in Naples within a few hours after Dörpfeld penned these words in Athens. The great pioneer Schliemann himself had lived in Athens for many years in a palatial house decorated in what he believed to be the Homeric style. There were to be found his daughter, Andromache; his son, Agamemnon; his porter, Bellerophon; and his footman, Telamon.

On Christmas Eve, 1890, Sienkiewicz, the author of *Quo Vadis*, was also in Naples, and he made the following remarks in a letter dated a few days later:[7]

As I sat [in the lobby of the hotel on the Piazza Umberto] that evening, a dying man was brought into the hotel. His head bowed down to his chest, eyes closed, arms hanging limp, and his face ashen, he was carried in by four people. This morbid group moved directly past the chair in which I sat, and after a while the manager of the hotel

7. See *Archaeology*, XI (1958), p. 218.

approached me and asked, "Do you know, Sir, who that sick man is?" "No." "That is the great Schliemann." Poor "great Schliemann!" He had excavated Troy and Mycenae, earned immortality for himself, and—was dying. Since that day the newspapers have brought even here to Cairo the news of his death. . . .

In 1893–1894 Dörpfeld came back to Troy to finish, as he thought, the work of Schliemann. The most important task was to attempt to learn more about the stratum in which the Mycenaean pottery had been found in 1890. In this, Dörpfeld was successful, for he discovered segments of the layer which he sought, and in this layer he was able to trace a large section of a great circuit wall of a town bigger than the Second City, a town whose pottery proved it to have been contemporary with Tiryns and Mycenae. This was named the Sixth City, and it was identified by Dörpfeld as Homeric Troy.

Because his excavations had been largely confined to the center of the mound, from which the Greeks and Romans had stripped all traces of the Sixth City to build the foundations for their structures, Schliemann had missed the Mycenaean remains at Troy which were preserved only on the slopes of the hill at a greater radius from the center where his efforts had been concentrated. Dörpfeld, as a result of the campaign of 1890, had new leads to follow. After the final dig of 1893–1894, these were his conclusions:[8]

1] The sixth stratum presents a stately acropolis, with many large buildings and an exceedingly strong circuit wall.

2] This acropolis flourished in the Mycenaean age, and hence it has first claim to be regarded as the Pergamos of Ilium celebrated by Homer.

3] The far more ancient acropolis of the second stratum antedated the Mycenaean age, and was repeatedly destroyed long before the time of the Trojan War.

Taking 1500–1000 B.C. as the approximate date of the Mycenaean epoch to which the Sixth City belongs, Dr. Dörpfeld offers the following tentative chronology of the Hissarlik settlements:

1. Lowest primitive settlement, with walls of small quarry stones and clay. Period (estimated) 3000–2500 B.C.

8. C. Tsountas, *The Mycenaean Age*, Boston 1897, pp. 368–369.

II. Prehistoric fortress, with strong walls and large brick buildings. Thrice destroyed and rebuilt. Monochrome pottery. Many objects of bronze, silver, and gold. Period (estimated) 2500–2000 B.C.

III–IV–V. Three prehistoric village settlements, built above the ruins of the second city. Houses of small stones and brick. Early Trojan pottery. Period about 2000–1500 B.C.

VI. Fortress of the Mycenaean age. Mighty circuit wall with great tower and stately houses of well-dressed stone. Advanced monochrome pottery of local fabric, and with it imported Mycenaean vases. The Homeric Pergamos of Troy. About 1500–1000 B.C.

VII–VIII. Village settlements, one of earlier, one of later, Hellenic times . . . From 1000 to the Christian era.

IX. Acropolis of Roman Ilium, with a famous temple of Athena and splendid marble buildings . . . Period from the beginning of the Christian era to A.D. 500.

For the next forty years, Dörpfeld's views went virtually unchallenged: there were nine "cities" at Troy, and the Sixth City was TROY. In the meantime, however, the world and archaeology moved on. At the beginning of the twentieth century, Sir Arthur Evans discovered the forgotten pre-Mycenaean civilization of the Minoans on the island of Crete. Synchronisms between Egypt and Crete were discovered which made it possible to date the Minoan finds with some precision, and connections between Crete and the Mycenaean Age in Greece were established which in turn enabled archaeologists to date Mycenaean pottery types with narrow limits. In archaeology concerned with Greece in the Bronze Age, pottery came to constitute the major criterion for dating the remains. One of the great contributors to this new technique was Carl Blegen of the University of Cincinnati, who subsequently conceived the idea of returning to Troy in order to review its pottery sequence. Between 1932–1938, a University of Cincinnati expedition dug at Troy with important results.

Professor Blegen's first report was made in 1933:[9]

The new excavations at Troy [beginning in April 1932] were undertaken with two definite objects in view. In the first place it

9. C. W. Blegen in *American Journal of Archaeology*, XXXVI (1932), pp. 431–433; 438–439. Quoted by permission of the publishers.

seemed both desirable and timely to make a fresh and thorough test of the stratification of the site. During the past generation a vast body of new knowledge has come to light bearing on the prehistoric cultures of the Eastern Mediterranean. The epoch-making discoveries of Sir Arthur Evans at Knossos and of the British, Italian, American, French and Greek excavators elsewhere in Crete, the supplementary researches of the German Archaeological Institute under Professors Karo and Müller at Tiryns, and of the British School under Dr. Wace at Mycenae, the intensified explorations in Central and Northern Greece, and Mr. Heurtley's systematic investigations in Macedonia, to mention only a few, have yielded an immense amount of new material from which it is possible to rebuild as a substantial and relatively orderly edifice the main structure of prehistoric Aegean Civilization. What relation does Troy bear to this structure and how do the successive "Cities" fit into the general scheme? That is a problem that has been much discussed in recent years, but which can only be definitely solved by a new and careful stratigraphic excavation. The evidence consists chiefly of the pottery and the other objects buried in the numerous layers of the accumulated deposit forming the mound at Hissarlik; and the definite determination from beginning to end of the Trojan ceramic sequence in much greater detail than hitherto possible from the earlier excavations has become a matter of paramount importance. A settlement of relatively great size and wealth, with a long history extending through the whole of the Bronze Age, and occupying a position almost unparalleled in its strategic aspect with reference to the main trade routes of the ancient world must have been a centre of traffic, an emporium with a flourishing business in exports and imports. The discovery of a few recognizable imported objects in an undisturbed context with local products may be expected to yield invaluable chronological evidence for dating the prehistoric cities more accurately than was hitherto possible. A meticulous re-examination of the stratified layers was consequently the principal object of the new excavations.

In the second place it seemed almost equally important to make an exhaustive search for the prehistoric tombs and cemeteries. No traces of such burials were brought to light in the previous excavations, although Schliemann in particular made repeated efforts to find them. It is possible that the early inhabitants of Troy had burial customs quite different from those practised in other contemporary centres of the Eastern Mediterranean. It may be, for example, that the dead were cremated in funeral pyres of such a nature that only scanty traces could have survived. But even if the latter supposition were true, some remains should still be recognizable, provided the place of incineration could be discovered, and they might shed no little light on the various stages in the evolution of culture in the Troad. A wide exploration of the whole district about Troy in the hope of finding the prehistoric tombs was thus set as the second object of the Expedition.

A third object, that of following the remaining circuit of the walls of Troy VI, the portions unexplored by Dörpfeld, was also conceived. Dörpfeld himself was still alive and vigorous, and . . .

Professor Dörpfeld collaborated whole-heartedly with the Expedition, spending four weeks with us at Troy and placing at our disposal without reserve all his knowledge of the site and its problems and all his experience in excavating. The advantage of having with us an expert familiar with almost every stone in the ruins . . . and who provided a direct link with Schliemann and his pioneer excavations can only be inadequately acknowledged . . . It seemed peculiarly fitting that he was thus enabled to celebrate at Troy in 1932 the fifty year jubilee of his active connection with the site; and the members of the expedition will long cherish in memory the pleasure and the privilege of being present on that occasion.

The reexamination of the stratigraphy of Troy was conducted on several "islands," or sections of the mound left unexcavated by Schliemann and Dörpfeld in order to indicate where the original ground level had been at the time the excavations had commenced in 1870. These were now slowly and carefully sliced off, layer by layer, inch by inch.

Among the areas left undug by Schliemann and Dörpfeld within the walls of the citadel, two were chosen for excavation because they seemed to offer the greatest likelihood of giving, when taken together, the complete sequence of strata that make up the mound. One of these was a tall pinnacle-like mass of earth left standing some 8 m. high inside the walls of the Second City . . . Here it seemed certain that we could count on finding undisturbed layers of the First, Second, Third, Fourth, and Fifth Cities . . . The second area lay farther south, inside and over the wall of the Sixth City, where we judged we could almost certainly find intact layers belonging to the Ninth, Eighth, Seventh and Sixth Cities and perhaps also the Fifth, Fourth and Third.

In the second area, beneath a dump of earth from Schliemann's excavations, four levels of occupation were recognized.

1] The uppermost layer clearly belongs to the Roman period. In the northern part of the trench two massive foundation walls appeared . . . The eastern ends of walls A and IX*b* had been demolished apparently in Byzantine times, when a deep trench seems to have been dug through the deposit from north to south. In the earth filling this trench were recovered Hellenistic coins and sherds, many architectural fragments of marble of the Doric and Ionic orders . . . Roman pottery and coins, sherds of yellow glazed Byzantine ware and Byzantine coins. . . .

2] The next layer of habitation, occupying a terrace at 1.25 m. below our bench mark, in the western part of the cutting, and the ground below it at 1.75 m. on the eastern side, may be assigned to the late prehistoric age . . . Three hearths were found, and there was also a large pit, or *bothros* . . . which contained many stones and numerous potsherds . . . The pottery from this layer was almost all a good gray ware with a polished surface, yellow and red wares being represented only scantily in coarse fabrics.

3] Next in order came what seemed to be a deep complicated layer in which three successive stages could be recognized . . . Floors came to light at *ca.* 2 m. . . . 2.30 m. and 2.35 m. . . . Yet other floors were encountered at 2.50 m. and 2.60 m. . . . A bothros had been cut through the floor found at 2.50 m., and in it was discovered burnt debris presumably from the earlier floor, including two complete vases and some potsherds. The latter comprised a fair number of Gray Minyan, some Mycenaean (Late Helladic III) and coarse ware. . . .

The extreme care of the excavators, the use of the precision afforded in measurement by the metric system, the technical language, the designations used for the pottery types—Gray Minyan, Late Helladic III—illustrate how the professional had replaced the amateur in archaeology, and what measure of maturity archaeology itself had attained since Schliemann's day. These reports were written for specialists; the layman would have to wait until the excavations had been completed and the results digested. Ultimately, he would be told in simple, untechnical terms all he needed to know.

By 1934 new theories about Troy were beginning to take shape. Although the excavations were revealing much about all layers, the stratigraphic analysis of the second island was to provide the most exciting news.[10]

A study of the ceramic sequence . . . leads logically to the conclusion that there was no break in continuity between Troy VI and VIIa; the periods are clearly to be regarded as representing merely two successive phases in the development of one and the same civilization. So far as we have hitherto observed, there is no evidence of a general conflagration marking the end of Troy VI. The city walls were certainly damaged and the houses probably demolished so that the settlement had to be rebuilt; but it seems likely that the destruction was occasioned by natural rather than political causes, and one is tempted to attribute the downfall of the Sixth City to a catastrophic earthquake. The handiwork of man may perhaps be seen, on the other hand, in the desolation stamping the ruins of Troy VIIa, when all the houses on the citadel were apparently gutted by a devastating fire, following which new cultural elements manifest themselves in the reconstructed town of VIIb.

Professor Dörpfeld has informed me [1935] that he is unable to accept the dating of Troy VI and VIIa which we proposed in our preliminary report for the season of 1934, and he has asked me to state his views. In that season we concluded from a study of the architectural and ceramic evidence that Troy VI came to its end, probably in a severe earthquake, not long after 1300 B.C.; that Troy VIIa, which immediately succeeded . . . maintained its existence for approximately a century until it was destroyed, doubtless by human agency, in a great conflagration in the early years of the twelfth century . . . Professor Dörpfeld holds that Troy VI was the seat of

10. C. W. Blegen in *American Journal of Archaeology* XXXIX (1935), pp. 16–17; p. 550. Quoted by permission of the publishers.

Priam, captured by Agamemnon; Troy VII*a*, the citadel of Aeneas and his descendants. . . .

But the evidence of earthquake was very clear in the walls and houses of Troy VI, and its pottery of Mycenaean manufacture could be dated to the fourteenth century B.C. The burning that brought to an end Troy VII*a* was also apparent; traces of it were discovered in other areas subsequently excavated at Troy. The pottery of Troy VII*a* could be dated, too. It ended at a date of around 1200 B.C., and this fitted very neatly with the traditional date for the destruction of Troy. In his final report published in 1958, Professor Blegen set the date for the destruction of Troy VII*a* at 1240 B.C.

The Cincinnati excavations at Troy were concluded in 1938, but the actual publication of the final report, which was composed of four huge volumes and two supplementary ones, did not begin until 1950; the fourth volume was issued in 1958. Not only had a new stratum (VII*a*) been identified as TROY, but many other discoveries had been made, not the least of which was that instead of the nine "cities" distinguished by the earlier excavators, the new investigation had resulted in the identification of more than *two score* strata on this site!

Decipherment

II

IN the study of the ancient Near East and prehistoric Greece the decipherment of the various ancient systems of writing and the reconstruction of dead languages has rivaled the archaeological discoveries in importance. The decipherment of the cuneiform, for example, made available new literary sources that illuminated the history, literature, political institutions, and the religious, economic, social, and scientific activities of the Near East in ways that the Old Testament or the writings of the Greeks and Romans could never have done.

We sometimes forget that any system of writing is a purely arbitrary affair, based upon convention. We could use the dots and dashes of the Morse code for writing just as easily as we use our alphabet. The alphabet, as a matter of fact, is not a particularly natural system of writing; it is a late development which had its origin in a kind of shorthand devised by professional scribes about 3500 years ago, at least a thousand years after the original invention of writing. It is instructive that, even after it began to have a limited use in Syria and Palestine, it took the alphabet another millennium to displace its competitors in the Near East, and we may be sure that there were generations of diehards who condemned the alphabet as new fangled, a lazy man's system that would never last.

The earliest kinds of writing in the world—in Mesopotamia, in Egypt, in the Indus valley, and later in China and Middle America—all seem to stem from simple picture writing. Then they moved to an ideographic stage in which characters were used to symbolize actions and concepts. Some systems of writing eventually became at least partially phonetic; for example, they employed certain characters to designate sounds. Now the curious thing about the older systems of writing was that very often they might use the same character or sign in three different ways: sometimes as a pictograph, sometimes as an ideographic sign, and sometimes as a phonetic character. In Sumerian, for example, the same sign might be used as a pictograph to denote the sun; ideographically, to mean "day"; and phonetically, to represent the sound "ou."

Some of the early systems of writing were borrowed and adapted for writing languages other than those for which they had been devised. To cite one example: when the Semites in Babylonia began to use the Sumerian cuneiform characters to write the various dialects of Akkadian, they made a number of changes. They retained for ordinary use only a few of the hundreds of pictographs and ideographic signs that had been created by the Sumerians. Instead, the Semites made greater use of phonetic characters in order to "spell out," or vocalize, words. Many of the pictographs and ideographs that *were* retained, however, were not radically changed in physical form, but they were read as Semitic rather than Sumerian words. The Sumerian sign for "king," which the Sumerians would read as *lugal* (the word for king in Sumerian), was read as *sharrum* (the Semitic word for king). By analogy, if people today were still using the cuneiform, we would read this sign, not as *lugal* or *sharrum*, but as *king*; the Romans would have read it *rex*; the French, *roi*; the Greeks, *basileus*. The same kind of thing happened when the Japanese borrowed the Chinese system of writing. The pictograph for "pine tree" would be read *shŏ* by the Chinese, and *matsu* by the Japanese.

As time passed, the tendency to write phonetically became more pronounced, and a new kind of writing, the *syllabary*, appeared. In this a limited number of characters represented the syllables necessary to write a given language more or less phonetically. The first syllabaries seem to have originated in Asia Minor just after 2000 B.C. Subsequently, the idea of syllabic writing was diffused to Cyprus, Crete, and Greece during the second millennium B.C.

By 1200 B.C. four great systems of writing were coexistent in the ancient civilized world:

1] the cuneiform, in Babylonia, Assyria, Asia Minor, Syria, and Palestine;

2] the Egyptian system, mostly confined to Egypt itself;

3] the syllabaries (Hieroglyphic Hittite, Minoan and its derivatives, and a few lesser varieties) in Asia Minor, Syria, Cyprus, Crete, and Greece; and

4] the alphabet, in Palestine and Syria. Furthermore, until very near the end of the pre-Christian era, all these systems continued to be employed in the ancient world. Thus, when the scholars of modern times wished to make use of the hundreds of thousands of documents in these scripts which archaeological research turned up, it was necessary to decipher these scripts and to reconstruct the underlying languages, most of which were extinct.

The Decipherment of the Cuneiform

From perhaps the second century B.C. to the nineteenth century A.D., the secret of reading the cuneiform was lost. As a matter of fact, there was even some doubt during that long period whether the strange arrow- or wedge-shaped characters had ever been used for writing. Yet cuneiform inscriptions were encountered over a wide area; early modern travelers from the seventeenth century onward reported seeing them not only in Mesopotamia but also in Iran, Asia Minor, and Syria. The fact that the characters were associated with relief sculpture and with other monuments suggested, at least, that they must be part of a system of writing. It was also noted that there were apparently different varieties of cuneiform. In Persia, for example, three distinct types were often found on the same monument, and it was suspected that three different languages might be represented of which one was very likely Old Persian.

The initial, but not the complete, decipherment of the cuneiform was accomplished at the beginning of the nineteenth century by a German schoolmaster named George Grotefend. Unfortunately, he was unable to arrive at a complete solution, and his later work was marred by wild guesses that cost him the confidence of people who thought at first that he was on the right track. The following passage from Rich's *Second Memoir on Babylon* (1818) shows Grotefend at the peak of his fame:[1]

The cuneiform, or, as it is sometimes called, the arrow-headed character, baffled the ingenuity of the decypherer till Dr. Grotefend of Frankfort, undeterred by the ill-success of his predecessors, applied himself to the task with a judgement and resolution which secured success . . . Dr. Grotefend who professes to be the decypherer rather than the translator of the cuneiform inscriptions, and who engages merely to open the way to those whose attention has been much devoted to the study of the ancient languages of Persia, has however succeeded in translating some of the inscriptions on the ruins of Persepolis, and one from those of Pasargadae. He observes that there are three varieties of those inscriptions, distinguished from each other by the greater complications of the characters formed by the radical signs of a wedge (or arrow) and an angle. Each inscription is repeated in all three species. The first or simplest species decyphered by Dr. Grotefend is in Zend, the language of Ecbatana, and there are grounds for believing the remaining ones are translations into the languages of the other capitals of the Persian Empire, Susa and Babylon. This conjecture acquires force from the fact of one of the species of cuneiform writing discovered at Babylon corresponding, or nearly so, with one of the Persepolitan species.

After Grotefend's studies bogged down, the work was continued by others with the final success being achieved by Sir Henry Rawlinson in 1846. The story of Rawlinson's solution of the puzzle is an interesting one and well worth retelling.

Sir Henry Rawlinson was a British army officer who had spent much time in the Near East. He knew modern Persian and other Oriental languages, and he became intensely interested in Near Eastern anti-

1. C. J. Rich, *Second Memoir on Babylon*, London 1818.

quities. As a military attache in Persia in the 1830's, he had ample time and opportunity to visit Persepolis and other ancient sites. Further, his experience with military codes and ciphers no doubt gave him confidence that he could answer the riddle of the cuneiform.

While there were many visible cuneiform inscriptions in Persia, most of them were very short, consisting of only a few characters. Without knowing much about what Grotefend had already done, Rawlinson was able to duplicate Grotefend's performance in deciphering a few personal names in the inscriptions, but he realized that his chances of real success would be much greater if he could have access to a long text which would give him ample opportunity to test, and ultimately to substantiate, his assumptions. A very lengthy inscription was known to exist, not in ancient Persia proper, but in the mountains on the caravan route between Hamadan and Baghdad. There, high up on a cliff on the face of a mountain called Bisitun, was a panel of sculptured figures accompanied by many lines of cuneiform in the same three scripts which also appeared on the monuments of Persia.

The Bisitun texts and its sculptures were very famous. The ancient Greek historian, Diodorus Siculus, attributed the monument to Semiramis, a legendary Assyrian queen, and later European travelers had had various ideas about the meaning of the Bisitun Rock and its sculptured figures. Some were sure that the figures represented the lost tribes of Israel, while others claimed that Jesus and the Apostles must be represented there. It is well worth noting at this point that people tend to interpret the unknown in terms of the known—or what they think they know. Since the Bisitun inscriptions were not in Greek or Latin, it was assumed that they belonged to the preclassical period, and the logical thing was to refer them to the age of the Old Testament. Such hypotheses might still be found in the Sunday Supplements if the positive identification of the figures had not been made through the decipherment of the cuneiform.

Early in the 1830's Rawlinson resolved to make copies of the Bisitun inscription. To climb up to the ledge where the sculptures may be seen at close range is not easy, but at that point the real trouble begins. This may be illustrated by reciting only one of Rawlinson's adventures:[2]

To copy part of the text he stood upon a native ladder, precariously

2. L. W. King and R. C. Thompson, *The Sculptures and Inscription of Darius*, London 1907.

balanced on a twelve-inch ledge, with a sheer drop of several hundred feet behind him . . .

One steadies the body against the rock with the left arm, while the left hand holds the notebook and the right hand is employed with the pencil. In this position I copied all of the upper inscriptions, and the interest of the occupation entirely did away with any sense of danger.

To reach the recess which contains the Scythic translation . . . is a matter of far greater difficulty. On the left side of the recess alone is there any footledge whatever; on the right hand . . . the face of the rock presents a sheer precipice, and it is therefore necessary to bridge this intervening space . . . With ladders of sufficient length, a bridge of this sort can be constructed without difficulty, but my first attempt to cross the chasm was unfortunate, for having previously shortened my only ladder in order to gain access to the upper Persian legends, I found that when I brought my ladder to the recess it was not sufficiently long to lie flat on the footledge beyond. One side of the ladder alone would reach to the nearest point of the ledge, and as it would have tilted over if a person had tried to cross in that position, I changed it from a horizontal to a vertical direction—the upper side resting firmly on the rock at its two ends and the lower hanging over the precipice—I prepared to cross walking on the lower side and holding to the upper side with my hands. If the ladder had been a compact article, this mode of crossing, though far from comfortable, would have been practicable, but the Persians merely fit in the bars of their ladders without pretending to clench them, and I had hardly begun to cross over when the vertical pressure forced the bars out of their sockets and the lower unsupported side of the ladder went crashing down over the precipice. Hanging to the upper side with my hands. . . .

In spite of these and other difficulties, Rawlinson managed to copy most of the great Bisitun inscription. He failed to get it all, but he got enough to prepare a paper which was read before the Royal Asiatic Society of London in 1839. At that time he planned to publish his paper in the *Transactions* of the Society for 1839, but, as he worked over the material, he realized that his translation might be improved by a more profound knowledge of philology.

The progress of the work was necessarily slow, but it was constant and uniform; and I might still have hoped to publish the Memoir in its amended form in the spring of 1840, had not circumstances, over which I had no control . . . arrested my inquiries in mid-career . . . Let it suffice to say that my services were called into activity by the Government, that I was suddenly transferred from the lettered seclusion of Baghdad to fill a responsible and laborious office in Afghanistan . . . But the years rolled on, and in December, 1843, I found myself again in Baghdad . . . [While a third version of the original memoir was in the process of preparation, Rawlinson made another visit to Bisitun in 1845] in which I succeeded in copying out the whole of the Persian writing at that place, and a very considerable portion also of the Median and Babylonian transcripts. I will not speak here of the dangers or difficulties of the enterprise. They are such as any person with ordinary nerves may encounter; but they are such, at the same time, as have alone prevented the inscriptions from being long ago presented to the public by some of the numerous travelers who have wistfully contemplated them at a distance.[3]

   To come to the problems of decipherment, it may be said at the outset that in all problems of this kind there are two important factors: analysis and assumption. An analysis of the Bisitun and other Persian texts had shown that three different kinds of cuneiform writing were employed, and it was therefore assumed that the same thing was being said in three different languages. Further analysis showed that one of the three varieties of writing was simpler than the other two: its characters were less complicated in form and fewer in number. As a matter of fact, just over two score characters were employed by this simplest type, while hundreds of different signs were used by the other two. This encouraged the assumption that the least complicated system was alphabetic in nature; the other two might belong to some system like the Egyptian in which there were pictographs, ideographs, and phonetic characters. Furthermore, the simplest type was most common in Persia, while one of the others seemed to have its home in Babylonia. Rawlinson therefore decided to work first on the simplest form which his earlier tests had suggested was a kind of alphabet with an underlying Persian dialect.
   An analysis of the assumed Old Persian text from Bisitun led to

3. Rawlinson in the *Journal of the Royal Asiatic Society*, X (1847).

other assumptions. One character, for example, in some inscriptions a crescent and in others an oblique wedge, occurred much more often than any other. This was assumed (correctly) to be a word divider. Then, it was noticed that in one section near the beginning of the Persian text, there were a number of repeated sequences, or words, which were assumed to be personal names, place names, or titles. This was on the analogy of Greek and Roman titulature and modern usage in the Near East, where a person might be styled, so-and-so, son of so-and-so, king of kings, defender of the faith, and so on.

All these assumptions encouraged a further hypothesis: namely, that the texts must belong to the period of the Achaemenid dynasty in Persia, the days of the Old Persian Empire (550–330 B.C.). Of the three great empires of ancient times known to have been centered in Persia, the alphabetic inscriptions of the Parthians and the Sassanians had already been identified, so there remained only the Achaemenid which also was known from the classical Greek authors to have had its capital at Persepolis.

At this point another factor was brought into play to supplement analysis and assumption. This was collateral information. Herodotus and other classical writers had preserved lists of the Achaemenid kings as well as some genealogical facts. There was Cyrus, the founder of the empire; then came his son and successor, Cambyses, who was followed by a distant cousin, Darius the Great. Darius was succeeded by his son, Xerxes; then came Artaxerxes—and so on, down to Darius III, who was overcome by Alexander the Great. Herodotus (VII, 11) gave the genealogy of Xerxes:

> For let me not be thought the child of Darius, the son of Hystaspes, the son of Arsames, the son of Ariaramnes, the son of Teispes . . . the son of Achaemenes, if I take not vengeance on the Athenians.

In his original memoir of 1839, Rawlinson said:

> It was in the year 1835 that I first undertook the investigation of the cuneiform character; I was at that time only aware that Professor Grotefend had decyphered some of the names of the early sovereigns of the house of Achaemenes, but in my isolated position at Kermanshah, on the western frontier of Persia, I could neither obtain a copy of his alphabet, nor could I discover what particular inscriptions he had examined. The first materials which I submitted to analysis were

the sculptured tablets of Hamadan . . . These tablets consist of two trilingual inscriptions, engraved by Darius [son of Hystaspes], and by his son Xerxes; they commence with the same invocation . . . they contain the same enumeration of the royal titles, and the same statement of paternity and family; and, in fact, they are identical, except in the names of the kings and in those of their respective fathers. When I proceeded, therefore, to compare and interline the two inscriptions . . . I found that the characters coincided throughout, except that in certain particular groupes, and it was only reasonable to suppose that the groupes which were thus brought out and individualized must represent proper names. I further remarked, that there were but three of these distinct groupes in the two inscriptions; for the groupe which occupied the second place in one inscription, and which, from its position, suggested the idea of its representing the name of the father of the king who was there commemorated, corresponded with the groupe which occupied the first place in the other inscription, and thus not only served determinately to connect the two inscriptions together, but, assuming the groupes to represent proper names, appeared also to indicate a genealogical succession. The natural inference was that in these three groupes of characters, I had obtained the proper names belonging to three successive generations of the Persian monarchy; and it so happened that the first three names of Hystaspes, Darius, and Xerxes, which I applied at hazard to the three groupes, according to the succession, proved to answer in all respects satisfactorily and were, in fact, the true identifications.

It would be fatiguing to detail the gradual progress which I made in the inquiry during the ensuing year. The collation of the first two paragraphs of the great Behistun Inscription with the tablets of Elwend supplied me, in addition to the names of Hystaspes, Darius, and Xerxes, with the native forms of Arsames, Ariaramnes, Teispes, Achaemenes, and Persia . . . and thus enabled me to construct an alphabet which assigned the same determinant values to eighteen characters. . . .

In order to understand the general process of decipherment, we ourselves may select the "second paragraph" of the Bisitun inscription—lines 4–6—where a striking number of repeated sequences occur. From these, we may make our own analysis.

In Chart I the material is so arranged as to show the sequences. The oblique wedges, the word dividers, have been circled. Each word has been assigned a letter, and examination of the chart will show that the following sequence of words emerges:

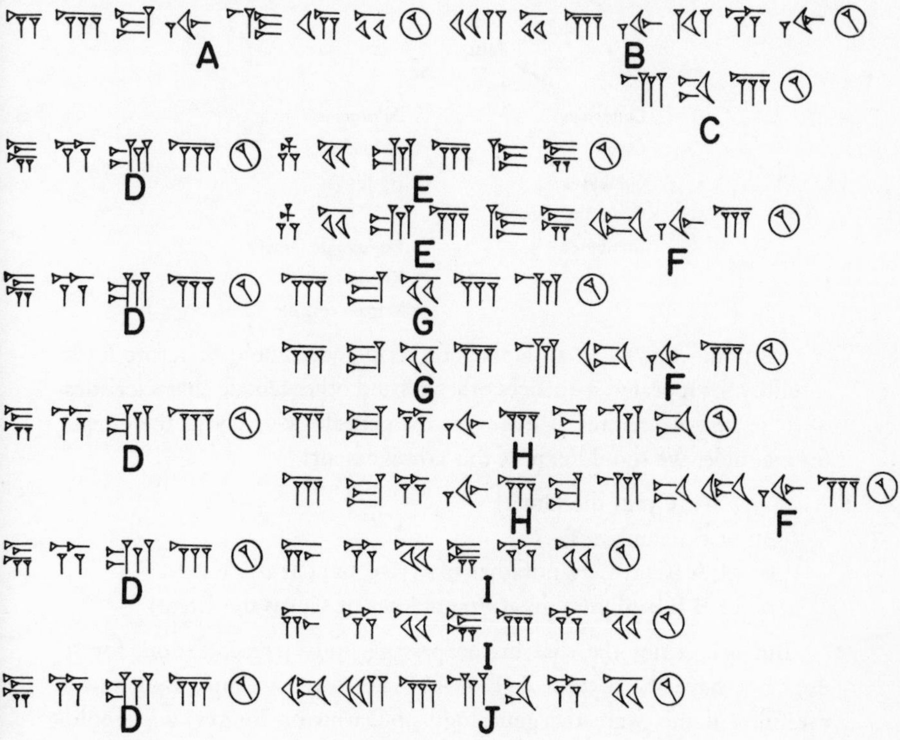

A   B

C

D   E

E   F

D   G

G   F

D   H

H   F

D   I

I

D   J

A-B-C
D-E
   E plus suffix F
D-G
   G plus suffix F
D-H
   H plus suffix F
D-I
   I
D-J

Now, if we assume as Rawlinson did, that this section contains some kind of a genealogical list, it is very likely that words **E, G, H, I,** and **J** are personal names. The genealogies of the Achaemenids were known to be:

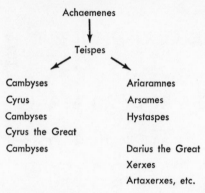

Assuming this to be an alphabetic script, we should therefore look carefully for repeated sequences of letters and other telltale characteristics of these personal names. If this were the genealogy of Cyrus the Great, for example, we should expect this arrangement:

A (Cyrus the Great)
son of **B** (Cambyses)
son of **A** (Cyrus, grandfather of Cyrus the Great)
son of **B** (Cambyses, great grandfather of Cyrus the Great)

But this is not the case in the passage under consideration, for it does not have the pattern **A-B-A-B.** Therefore, we must look more carefully. If this were the genealogy of Darius or Xerxes, we should find there three names containing the letters **AR,** as in **DAR**ius, **AR**sames and **ARIAR**amnes. In our text, of course, words **A, G,** and **H** display these patterns. We shall therefore make the following assumptions:

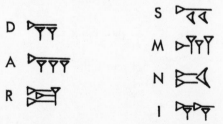

Next, we shall substitute the letters of our modern alphabet in the text in accordance with the assumptions we have made. This will give us:

A	B	C
DAR	. SA . . I .	MNA

D	E	
. I . A	. S . A . .	
		F
	. S . A . .	. . A

D	G	
. I . A	ARSAM	
		F
	ARSAM	. . A

D	H	
. I . A	ARI . ARMN	
		F
	ARI . ARMN	. . A

D	I	
. I . A	. IS . IS	
	. IS . AIS	

D	J
. I . A	. . AMNIS

This shows that we are on the right track. In line 1 we have DAR (Darius), and Arsames and Ariaramnes appear to be emerging in G and H. The . IS . IS of I suggests Teispes just as . . AMNIS in J ought to give us Achaemenes. If we assume a value of P for ⬚ in E and I, we shall have parts of Teispes and Hystaspes, while ⬚ in J must be K.

Further work will disclose that the Greek versions of the Persian proper names will have to be corrected to the appropriate Persian forms since Old Persian possessed sounds that were not present in Greek. It will also be discovered that this Persian script is not an alphabet, but a syllabary.

Rawlinson finally read this passage as:

Dar(a)yawush khshayathiya mana pita Vashtaspa Vashtaspahya pita Arshama Arshamahya pita Ariyaram(a)na Ariyaram(a)hya pita Chishpish Chishpaish pita Hakhamanish.

Today, it would be written:

D-A-RA-YA-VA-U-SH   X-SH-A-YA-TH-I-YA   MA-N-A
　　　　Darius　　　　　　　　　　(the) King　　　　　　my

P-I-T-A   VI-SH-T-A-S-PA   VI-SH-T-A-S-PA-H-Y-A
　father　　(was) Hystaspes　　　　　　　Hystaspes'

P-I-T-A   A-R-SH-A-MA   A-R-SH-A-MA-H-Y-A
　father　　(was) Arsames　　　　　Arsames'

P-I-T-A   A-R-I-Y-A-RA-M-NA   A-R-I-Y-A-RA-M-NA-H-Y-A
　father　　(was) Ariaramnes　　　　　　Ariaramnes'

P-I-T-A   CH-I-SH-P-I-SH   CH-I-SH-P-A-I-SH
　father　　(was) Teispes　　　　Teispes'

P-I-T-A   HA-X-A-M-N-I-SH
　father　　(was) Achaemenes

Note on pronunciation: **X** as in Greek *chi* or German *ch*;
　　　　　　　　　　　　CH as in English "cherry."

This section alone contained nearly one-half the phonetic characters in the Persian script, and Rawlinson was able to recover the remainder as he worked on through the Bisitun inscription aided by his studies of the Persian dialects and Sanscrit.

Rawlinson was modest about his achievements. In his memoir he gave credit to Grotefend as "being the first who opened a gallery into this rich treasure-house of antiquity." Moreover, he acknowledged the progress made by other scholars independently of his researches. Much, in fact, had been done between the time Rawlinson read his paper in 1839 and the final publication of his memoir in 1847.

As far as the public judgement is concerned in awarding to competitors the prize of originality, there can be little room either for confusion or embarrassment; for priority of announcement is held, I believe, in all cases to decide the question of priority of discovery. Individually also, so far from desiring to impugn the merits, or to contest the rights of others, I should be well content to rest my present claims on the novelty and interest of my translations . . . In the present case, then, I do put forth a claim to originality, as having been the first to present to the world a literal and, as I believe, a correct grammatical translation of nearly two hundred lines of cuneiform writing, a memorial of the time of Darius . . . the purport of which to the historian must, I think, be of fully equal interest with the peculiarities of its language to the philologist.

The Bisitun inscription, as it turned out, was set up by Darius the Great of Persia about 519 B.C. Its long text gave an account of how Darius came to the throne after the death of Cambyses and how he overcame the various pretenders and revolutionists who threatened to destroy the unity of the Persian Empire. This "apology of Darius" was very widely circulated throughout his realm. One copy in the Aramaic language and alphabet written on a papyrus was found far to the south in Egypt where it had been dispatched to a colony of Jewish mercenaries stationed by the first cataract of the Nile to guard the Egyptian frontier.

Once the Persian text of the Bisitun inscription had been translated, it was possible to turn to a study of the other two versions inscribed on the rock. One was correctly assumed to be Babylonian; but, although the Babylonian language was soon found to be closely related to Hebrew, the decipherment of the Babylonian version was difficult because its complex script was not essentially phonetic, like the Persian, but used characters that were pictographic and ideographic as well as phonetic. By the year 1850 great progress had been made, and the translation of the Babylonian led scholars directly into the Assyrian that Layard and Botta had found at Nimrud, Nineveh, and Khorsabad. The relative ease of this translation was due, of course, to the fact that the Babylonian and Assyrian languages were both Semitic and closely related.

The third version at Bisitun, the one which Rawlinson had called Median or Scythian, was the most difficult of all. The underlying language was, as Grotefend had guessed, the Elamite tongue, the language of Susa. Elamite belongs to a family of languages unrelated either to Persian, which is Indo-European, or to any of the Semitic languages. It is only within our generation that much progress has been made with Elamite. Elamite texts have always been few in number; this was why George Cameron, one of the few authorities on Elamite, returned to Bisitun in 1948 to make new copies and casts of the Elamite version. With modern equipment, he was able to get at large portions of the Elamite texts which had been inaccessible to Rawlinson a hundred years before.

As we have seen, Rawlinson's decipherment of the Persian text at Bisitun paved the way for the reading also of Babylonian and Assyrian. By 1856 all doubt that the cuneiform could be read was dispelled by a spectacular test. A half-dozen scholars were each given a copy of the same untranslated Assyrian text. Working independently, each made a translation which was then placed in a sealed envelope. At a given time all the envelopes were opened together and their contents compared. The results were amazing in the uniformity of the translations thus revealed.

This was by no means the end of the story, for it was soon discovered that the cuneiform system had been used by many different groups and for writing a variety of languages. Although the Semitic-speaking Babylonians and Assyrians used the cuneiform for hundreds of years, they were not, as people had originally supposed, the inventors of this kind of writing. The chief claimants for this honor are the Sumerians who were certainly using the cuneiform before 3000 B.C.

Sumerian, like Elamite, is a language long extinct; but Sumerian, unlike Elamite which may be related to some modern languages in Armenia and the Caucasus, cannot be connected with any known language, living or dead. The grammars and dictionaries found by Layard at Nineveh were, we now know, used by the Assyrian priests for reading Sumerian, but for a long time modern scholars entertained the idea that Sumerian was nothing more than a kind of secret writing used by the Babylonians. It is only in the twentieth century that decided progress in reading Sumerian has been made; it is still a difficult task to translate the texts satisfactorily.

The Sumerians, then, were probably the inventors of the cuneiform. Their invention was adopted and adapted by the Semitic-speaking tribes that entered Mesopotamia. The earliest known written Semitic language in Mesopotamia appears about 2350 B.C. It is called Old Akkadian. Next comes the Old Babylonian dialect of the Hammurabi period in the first half of the second millennium B.C., and the earliest forms of Assyrian also go back to about 1900 B.C. although most of the Assyrian texts come from a period a thousand years later.

Outside of Mesopotamia, the cuneiform was adopted by many other groups. Just before World War I, German excavators in central Asia Minor discovered the capital of the Hittite Empire which flourished during the second millennium B.C. Here were found many cuneiform tablets: some were Old Babylonian or Sumerian, but others could not be read at all. The script seemed familiar enough, but the texts made no sense until it was realized that the underlying language was a new one, Hittite, essentially an Indo-European tongue.

In the 1920's excavations near Kirkuk in Iraq at a site known in ancient times as Nuzi brought to light cuneiform tablets written in still another language, Hurrian, perhaps a distant relative of Elamite. The Hurrians, the Horites of the Old Testament, had once been a great people in northern Mesopotamia, but their existence had long since been forgotten until the discoveries at Nuzi. Hurrian was found to be a member of a separate language family—not Indo-European, not Semitic, not Sumerian.

Nor does this exhaust the catalog of groups which used the cuneiform. Greek appears in the cuneiform texts of Babylonia following the conquests of Alexander the Great. And research is still involved with another language that was written with the cuneiform script, for to the north of Assyria, up around Lake Van in Armenia, there lived in Assyrian times a people called the Urartians who borrowed the cuneiform system from their neighbors to the south. These Vannic inscriptions are available in some quantity, but they still await satisfactory translation.

The Decipherment of Egyptian Hieroglyphics

It is usually said that the Rosetta Stone, found by the French in Egypt in 1799, gave Jean François Champollion the clue which enabled him to decipher the hieroglyphs of Egypt in 1822. This is only partially correct: it was not the Rosetta Stone only that Champollion had to use in his decipherment, and his work was not done in a vacuum: his success was partly due to the previous discoveries of other scholars, not the least of whom was the brilliant and versatile English scientist and medical man, Dr. Thomas Young.

The Rosetta Stone, a slab of black basalt nearly four feet high and almost two and a half feet wide, bears a bilingual inscription which is written in three scripts: the Egyptian text is rendered in hieroglyphic and demotic, and the Greek text in the Greek alphabet. The top had been broken off so that while there were fifty-four lines of Greek and thirty-two of demotic, the hieroglyphic text was only fourteen lines in length. This was enough, however, to further decipherment by Champollion, once Young using the Greek text to decipher the demotic provided an Egyptian version that Champollion could use for work on the hieroglyphic text. Champollion's initial entry, nevertheless, was accomplished by using various other Egyptian texts which contained Greek and Roman personal names. There were many such texts known from the post-pharaonic period in Egypt; even the Rosetta Stone is late, for it was written in 195 B.C.

In his use of the personal names and titles to make his initial entry, Champollion followed the method which Grotefend had already used with the cuneiform and which Rawlinson was to employ with success later. Champollion and others had noticed on the Egyptian monuments inscribed with hieroglyphs that certain characters were enclosed in boxes, or cartouches, that set these groups of characters off from the remainder of the text. It was therefore assumed that these characters in the cartouches must "spell out" the names of rulers and gods. An obelisk bearing an inscription related to that on the Rosetta Stone was known to contain the names of Ptolemy, a Greco-Egyptian king, and his queen, Cleopatra.

Now, **PTOLEMAIOS** and **KLEOPATRA**, the Greek forms of these names, have several letters in common: **P, T, O, L, E,** and **A.** If one could find the cartouches of Ptolemy and Cleopatra, one might identify them by the fact that the first letter in Ptolemy's name ought to reappear as the fifth letter in Cleopatra's. Thus one could set the letters from the two cartouches side by side and make assumptions about the phonetic values. Without reproducing the letters in the cartouches, we may simply diagram the process of decipherment by giving numbers to the individual characters:

PTOLEMAIOS   1 - 2 - 3 - 4 - 5 - 6 - 7
KLEOPATRA   8 - 4 - 9 - 3 - 1 - 10 - 11 - 12 - 10
                     P T O L M
                     K L E O P A T R A

Primary assumption	Secondary assumption	No assumption
1 P	2 T	6
3 O	5 M	7
4 L	8 K	
10 A	9 E	
	11 T?	
	12 R	

This could be tested on another name, ALEXANDROS, and also on still another queen's name, BERENIKE

ALEXANDROS   10 - 4 - 13 - 7 - 9 - 14 - 11 - 12 - 15
                     A L   S E   T   R

New assumptions 13 K; 14 N; 15 S

BERENIKE   16 - 12 - 14 - 6 - 17
                     R   N   I

New assumptions 16 B; 17 K

Then there were two titles of the Roman period. Their Greek forms were AUTOKRATOR and KAISAROS

AUTOKRATOR   A - 18 - T - A - K - R - T - R
                     10 - 18 - 11 - 10 - 17 - 12 - 11 - 12
KAISAROS   13 - 6 - 15 - 4 - 15
                     K I S L S

As a consequence of these simple operations the phonetic values for the following characters could be confirmed:

1 P; 3 O; 4 L; 6 I; 7 S; 9 E; 10 A; 11 T;
12 R; 13 K; 14 N; 15 S; 17 K

and the remainder were virtually certain:

2 T; 5 M; 8 K; 16 B; 18 U

Moreover, this accounted for about one half of the so-called Egyptian alphabet. The real problem lay with working out the values for the pictographic and ideographic characters, and this was where the Rosetta Stone was most helpful since the content of the inscription was known from the Greek and the Egyptian text known from the demotic.

The Decipherment of Minoan Linear B

There have been other feats of decipherment since the time of Champollion and Rawlinson. The simultaneous decipherment of the Ras Shamra (Ugaritic) alphabet by Bauer and Dhorme in 1932 was a remarkable achievement. Nevertheless, Michael Ventris' decipherment of the Minoan Linear B in 1952 is generally considered—and justly so—to be one of the greatest accomplishments of its kind. This matter will not be discussed here, since accounts of Ventris' work are easily available,[4] but several points of importance should be noted:

1] Where Champollion and Rawlinson could treat their scripts as if they were alphabetic—though they were not—the Linear B was a syllabary. Furthermore, the underlying language could not be assumed to be known, and thus Ventris did not have the same advantage as Champollion and Rawlinson. As it turned out the language underlying Linear B was Greek, but this was by no means apparent. Ventris first assumed that he was dealing with Etruscan. When this led nowhere, he made no further assumptions about the language until his analyses had reached what was virtually a final stage.

2] The consequences of the decipherment of Linear B have been fully as important for historical and linguistic studies as the solutions of the riddles of the hieroglyphs and the cuneiform. The Linear B texts show the Greeks as the dominant people in Greece in the Mycenaean Age. Moreover, the texts have revealed much about governmental organization, economic life, and religious beliefs in the Mycenaean period that could never have been learned from the archaeological sources or from the literary accounts of the classical authors.

4. J. Chadwick, *The Decipherment of Linear B*, New York 1958.

New chapters are still to be written in the history of the decipherment of ancient scripts. That of the Indus Valley cannot be read as yet. Minoan Linear A is not completely *deciphered*, and its underlying language remains unidentified, despite extravagant claims to the contrary. The Phaistos Disc, the Minoan hieroglyphic script, the hieroglyphic syllabary from Byblos, and several scripts from Asia Minor and Cyprus are still in the category of unfinished business.

A Few Basic Facts about Ancient Writing

We are used to alphabetic writing and word division, but these are both late developments and not as essential to successful written communication as we sometimes assume. Word division, especially, is a mere convention to which we have become accustomed; with a little practice, we could get along without it. The cost of printing could be greatly reduced if we were to dispense with word division and the use of characters for the vowels.

T H B R W N T V R T H M N T N
does not take up nearly as much space as
THE BEAR WENT OVER THE MOUNTAIN

The great advantage of our alphabet as compared with some other scripts, of course, is that we have to learn only twenty-six characters in order to write it. A syllabary may consist of anywhere from forty-five to one hundred and thirty characters, and a more complex system ordinarily requires hundreds of signs.

An alphabet, as we know it, is a phonetic system, and it needs to be adapted to the phonetic patterns of the language for which it is to be used. At first the Romans could write Latin with only twenty characters: ABCDEFHIKLMNOPQRSTVX. The V served for both U, a vowel, and W, a consonant. The Romans wrote CAIVS IVLIVS CAESAR, VICTVS, VIRTVS, and so forth. Later phonetic changes in Latin led them to adopt G, and, as they borrowed Greek words, they added Y and Z—as in ZEPHYRVS. The Greeks at Athens used only twenty-one letters for a long time: *eta* (H) was employed as an aspirate (h). Later, when the Ionic alphabet was adopted, the alphabet contained twenty-four letters: *eta* became long ε, and the aspirate was dropped; omega was added for long o; and *xi* and *psi* were the other two additions. Since *eta* as an aspirate was now omitted, this gave a total of twenty-four letters. In some of the "West Greek" alphabets, there were two letters not found in the Ionic: *digamma* for w, and *koppa* for q.

As we ordinarily encounter it, a syllabary is a system which has characters for various consonant-vowel combinations, and also a set for the vowels alone. As an example of a syllabary we may take the one used on the island of Cyprus in classical times (sixth and seventh centuries B.C.). It employed between sixty and sixty-five characters. A descendant of Minoan, or perhaps a relative, this syllabary was originally used for writing an unknown language with a limited phonetic pattern, but it was also employed for writing Greek. The Cypriote syllabary had separate characters for the five vowels (a, e, i, o, u) and for various consonant-vowel combinations: **KA, KI, KE, KO, KU, TA, TI, TE, TO, TU,** and so on. The script was not well adapted for writing Greek because it lacked consonant-vowel combinations involving **B, D, G, TH, PH, PS, KS,** or Greek *chi*. Furthermore, as in the Minoan script, it was customary to omit N before T. Thus, Greek *agathos* and *akanthos* would both be written **A-KA-TO-SE.** Such spellings as **SA-TA-SA-TO-RO** for Stasander or **NI-KO-TA-MO** for Nikodamos or **NI-KO-KE-LE-O-SE** for Nikokleos seem a little awkward, but the Cypriote script would not be completely satisfactory for English, either:

MA-RI   HA-TA   LI-TI-LE   LA-MA-PA

But in Minoan Linear B (Mycenaean), which did not distinguish between L and R, we would find no great improvement:

MA - RI   HA - DA   RI - TI - RE   RA - MA - PA

Turning to the more complex systems of writing, we may compare the opening lines of the Bisitun Inscription of Darius as they were written in the Persian syllabary and in the Babylonian with the way in which they might have been written in other scripts and languages.

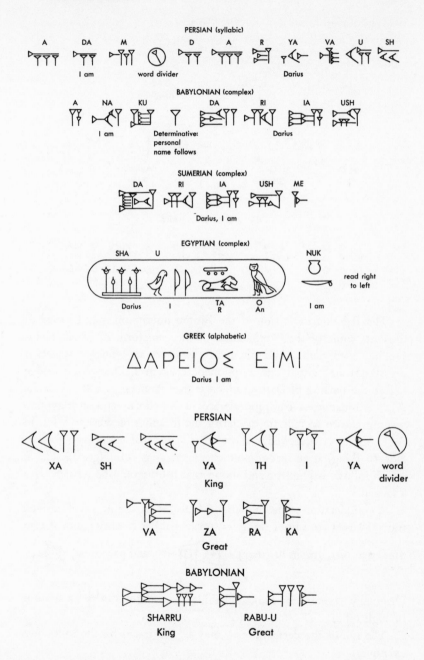

PERSIAN (syllabic)

A DA M word divider D A R YA VA U SH

I am Darius

BABYLONIAN (complex)

A NA KU DA RI IA USH

I am Determinative: personal name follows Darius

SUMERIAN (complex)

DA RI IA USH ME

Darius, I am

EGYPTIAN (complex)

SHA U NUK

Darius I TA R O An I am read right to left

GREEK (alphabetic)

ΔΑΡΕΙΟΣ ΕΙΜΙ

Darius I am

PERSIAN

XA SH A YA TH I YA word divider

King

VA ZA RA KA

Great

BABYLONIAN

SHARRU RABU-U

King Great

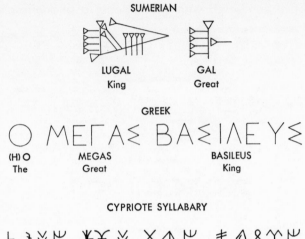

The Babylonian version of the Bisitun inscription may be used to illustrate some of the complexities of the cuneiform in which pictographic, ideographic, and phonetic characters are mingled together. **a-na-ku** (I am) employs three phonetic characters. The vertical wedge before the spelling of Darius, which is also phonetic, is a *determinative*. A determinative, a common device in cuneiform and in Egyptian writing is used to indicate or clarify the meaning of what follows. In this case the vertical wedge shows that a personal name is to follow. **Sharru** (king) is an ideographic character, as is **rabu** (great). The u which follows is phonetic and shows that **rabu** should be written with a long u.

A consideration of the Sumerian **lugal-gal** (great king) will be even more instructive. **Lugal** (king = great-man) is a compound of two Sumerian pictographs **lu** (man) and gal (great) .

Originally **lu** must have looked like this and gal was , a symbol of high office.

The use of the determinative may be illustrated by the following examples:

Determinative combined with shur (alone, a phonetic character)

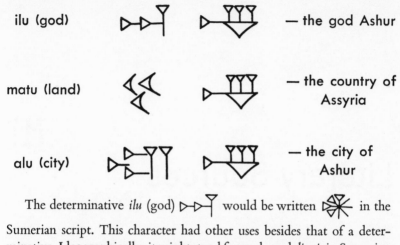

ilu (god) — the god Ashur

matu (land) — the country of Assyria

alu (city) — the city of Ashur

The determinative *ilu* (god) ▷▷⌐ would be written ◁✳ in the Sumerian script. This character had other uses besides that of a determinative. Ideographically, it might stand for god, read *dingir* in Sumerian and *ilu* in Babylonian, or for sky (*an* in Sumerian; *shamu* in Babylonian). If we encountered ▷▷⌐ ▷▷⌐ we might read it *dingir an* in Sumerian or *ilu Anu* in Babylonian: this means "the god An (or Anu)," who was the sky god. Unfortunately, these two characters in combination might simply means "gods" since the plural was sometimes indicated by duplicating a sign. Thus ⧼ (land) when doubled ⧼ ⧼ would be read "lands." To come back to ilu ▷▷⌐, it also had a number of phonetic values: an, il, el, li, al, sa, and several more. Many times, only the context gives an indication of whether a sign is to be read as a pictograph, ideograph, or phonetically—and the appropriate phonetic reading will also depend on the context.

From this, it will be seen that the scripts we have labelled complex are truly so and require some practice before they can be easily read.

III

Literary Sources

IT is virtually axiomatic that one cannot accept a literary source at its face value. Some, of course, are more to be trusted than others, and we shall have occasion to examine this matter more fully later on. For the present, however, it will be sufficient to demonstrate that the classical authors did not always provide accurate information relating to the ancient history of the Near East. At the same time it can be shown how Near Eastern documents may be used to achieve more reliable historical reconstruction than might be possible through the classical writers alone.

The Tale of Gyges

The story of Gyges, the ancestor of Croesus and the founder of the last dynasty to reign in Lydia before the Persian conquest, is most familiar in the version given by Herodotus. Herodotus wrote in the second half of the fifth century B.C., and his account of Gyges was said to have been derived from the long-lost Lydian History of Xanthus (*c.* 450 B.C.). Xanthus was also supposed to have been the source for Nicolaus of Damascus (first century A.D.). Other accounts of importance relating to Gyges are to be found in Plato's *Republic*; the work of Justin, a Latin author of the second or third century A.D. who condensed a history by Pompeius Trogus (first century A.D.); a passage in Plutarch's *Greek Questions* (early second century A.D.); and a notice in Photius (ninth century A.D.) derived from Ptolemy Chennos (first century A.D.).[1]

HERODOTUS [1, 7–16]

The sovereignty of Lydia, which had belonged to the Heracleidae, passed into the family of Croesus, who were called Mermnadae, in the manner which I will now relate. There was a certain king of Sardis, Candaules by name, whom the Greeks called Myrsilus. He was a descendant of Alcaeus, son of Heracles. The first king of this dynasty was Agron, son of Ninus, grandson of Belus, and great-grandson of Alcaeus; Candaules, son of Myrsus, was the last. The kings who reigned before Agron sprang from Lydus, son of Atys, from whom the people of the land, called previously Maeonians, received the name of Lydians. The Heracleidae, descended from Heracles and the slave girl of Jordanus, having been entrusted by these princes with the management of affairs, obtained the kingdom by an oracle. Their rule endured for two and twenty generations of men, a space of five hundred and five years; during the whole of which period, from Agron to Candaules, the crown descended in the direct line from father to son.

Now it happened that this Candaules was in love with his own wife; and not only so, but thought her the fairest woman in the whole world. This fancy had strange consequences. There was in his body-guard a man who he specially favored, Gyges, the son of Dascylus. All affairs of greatest moment were entrusted by Candaules to this person, and to him he was wont to extoll the surpassing beauty of his wife. So matters went on for a while. At length, one day, Candaules, who was fated to end ill, thus addressed his follower: "I see thou dost not credit what I tell thee of my lady's loveliness; but come

1. The translations of the classical authors are those of George Rawlinson and K. F. Smith (see footnote 2).

now, since men's ears are less credulous than their eyes, contrive some means whereby thou mayest behold her naked." At this the other loudly exclaimed, saying, "What most unwise speech is this, master, which thou hast uttered? Wouldst thou have me behold my mistress when she is naked? Bethink thee that a woman, with her clothes, puts off her bashfulness? Our fathers, in time past, distinguished right and wrong plainly enough, and it is our wisdom to be taught by them. There is an old saying, 'Let each look at his own.' I hold thy wife for the fairest of all womankind. Only, I beseech thee, ask me not to do wickedly."

Gyges thus endeavored to decline the king's proposal, trembling lest some dreadful evil should befall him through it. But the king replied to him, "Courage, friend; suspect me not of the design to prove thee by this discourse; nor dread thy mistress lest mischief befall thee at her hands. Be sure I will so manage that she shall not even know that thou hast looked upon her. I will place thee behind the open door of the chamber in which we sleep. When I enter to go to rest she will follow me. There stands a chair close to the entrance, on which she will lay her clothes one by one as she takes them off. Thou wilt be able thus at thy leisure to peruse her person. Then, when she is moving from the chair toward the bed, and her back is turned on thee, be it thy care that she see thee not as thou passest through the doorway."

Gyges, unable to escape, could but declare his readiness. Then Candaules, when bedtime came, led Gyges into his sleeping chamber, and a moment after, the queen followed. She entered, and laid her garments on the chair, and Gyges gazed on her. After a while she moved toward the bed, and her back being then turned, he glided stealthily from the apartment. As he was passing out, however, she saw him, and instantly divining what had happened, she neither screamed as her shame impelled her, nor even appeared to have noticed aught, purposing to take vengeance upon the husband who had so affronted her. For among the Lydians, and indeed among the barbarians generally, it is reckoned a deep disgrace, even to a man, to be seen naked.

No sound or sign of intelligence escaped her at the time. But in the morning, as soon as day broke, she hastened to choose from among her retinue, such as she knew to be most faithful to her, and preparing them for what was to ensue, summoned Gyges into her presence. Now it had often happened before that the queen had desired to confer with him, and he was accustomed to come at her call. He therefore obeyed the summons, not suspecting that she knew aught of what had occurred. Then she addressed these words to him: "Take thy choice, Gyges, of two courses which are open to thee. Slay Candaules, and thereby become my lord, and obtain the Lydian throne, or die this moment in his room. So wilt thou not again, obeying all behest of thy master, behold what is not lawful for thee. It must needs be, that either he perish by whose counsel this thing was done, or thou, who sawest me naked, and so didst break our usages." At these words Gyges stood awhile in mute astonishment; recovering after a time, he earnestly besought the queen that she would not compel him to so hard a choice. But finding he implored in vain, and that necessity was indeed laid on him to kill or to be killed, he made a choice of life for himself, and replied by this inquiry: "If it must be so, and thou compellest me against my will to put my lord to death, come, let me hear how thou wilt have me set on him." "Let him be attacked," she answered, "on that spot where I was by him shown naked to you, and let the assault be made when he is asleep."

All then was prepared for the attack, and when night fell, Gyges, seeing that he had no retreat or escape, but must absolutely either slay Candaules, or himself be slain, followed his mistress into the sleeping room. She placed a dagger in his hand, and hid him carefully behind the selfsame door. Then Gyges, when the king had fallen asleep, entered privily into the chamber and struck him dead. Thus did the wife and kingdom of Candaules pass into the possession of Gyges, of whom Archilochus the Parian, who lived about the same time, made mention in a poem written in iambic trimeter verse.

Gyges was afterwards confirmed in the possession of the throne by an answer of the Delphic oracle. Enraged at the murder of their king, the people flew to arms, but after a while the partisans of Gyges came to terms with them, and it was agreed that if the Delphic oracle declared him king of the Lydians, he should reign; if otherwise, he should yield the throne to the Heraclides. As the oracle was given in his favor he became king. The Pythoness, however, added that, in the fifth generation from Gyges, vengeance should come for the Heraclides; a prophecy of which neither the Lydians nor their princes took any account till it was fulfilled. Such was the way in which the Mermnadae deposed the Heraclides, and themselves obtained the sovereignty.

When Gyges was established on the throne, he sent no small presents to Delphi, as his many silver offerings at the Delphic shrine testify. Besides this silver he gave a vast number of vessels of gold, among which the most worthy of mention are the goblets, six in number, and weighing altogether thirty talents, which stand in the Corinthian treasury, dedicated by him . . . Excepting Midas, son of Gordius, king of Phrygia, Gyges was the first of the barbarians whom we know to have sent offerings to Delphi. Midas dedicated the royal throne whereon he was accustomed to sit and administer justice, an object well worth looking at. It lies in the same place as the goblets presented by Gyges. The Delphians call the whole of the silver and the gold which Gyges dedicated, after the name of the donor, Gygian.

As soon as Gyges was king he made an inroad on Miletus and Smyrna, and took the city of Colophon. Afterwards, however, though he reigned eight and thirty years, he did not perform a single noble exploit. I shall therefore make no further mention of him, but pass on to his son and successor, Ardys.

Ardys took Priene and made war upon Miletus. In his reign the Cimmerians, driven from their homes by the nomads of Scythia, entered Asia and captured Sardis, all but the citadel. He reigned forty-nine years, and was succeeded by his son, Sadyattes, who reigned twelve years. At his death his son Alyattes mounted the throne.

This prince waged war with the Medes under Cyaxares, the grandson of Deioces, drove the Cimmerians out of Asia, conquered Smyrna, the Colophonian colony, and invaded Clazomenae.

NICOLAUS OF DAMASCUS

In the reign of Myrsos, Daskylos, the son of that Daskylos who had been assassinated by the king's father, fearing lest the Herakleidai would encompass his death also, fled to the Syrians above Sinope. There he married a woman of the country and had by her a son, Gyges. There lived in Sardis an uncle of Gyges' father. His name was Ardys. Having lost his children, Ardys went to king Sadyattes, asked for the recall of his nephew Daskylos and for permission to adopt him. The request was granted. Daskylos, however, preferred to remain where he was. But he sent in his place his son Gyges, at that time a youth of eighteen, remarkable for his size and beauty, a good soldier, and surpassing his equals in all things, but especially, in the management of arms and horses. These gifts and accomplishments soon recommended him to the king who made him one of his bodyguard. Shortly after, however, Sadyattes became suspicious of him and exposed him to all sorts of peril, and difficulties, being unwilling to destroy him openly, as he had no reasonable excuse. But inasmuch as Gyges performed all his tasks successfully the king forgot his former suspicions and gave him great estates.

Some time later Sadyattes decided to take Tudo to wife, the daughter of Arnossos who was king of Mysia and founder of the city of Ardynios in the plain of Thebe. When the time came for fetching the bride, Sadyattes put Gyges in a chariot and sent him after her. But while riding with her in the chariot he became enamoured of her and, not being able to restrain himself, undertook to seduce her. She, however, being disinclined to him fell into a furious rage, made all manner of threats and when she came to the king told him all. Whereat, the king was wroth and swore to kill Gyges the next day.

Now this was heard by a maid who was in the bedchamber at the time and, as she was deeply in love with Gyges, she immediately told him everything. Gyges went to all his friends during the night, confided the matter to them and, reminding them all of the curses which Ardys had called down upon the murderers of Daskylos, asked them to help him in his plan to kill the king.

Therefore, thinking that, under the circumstances, it was better to slay Sadyattes than be slain by him, and being assured of faithful friends to help him, Gyges broke into the palace, sword in hand, and, entering the chamber, the door of which was opened for him by the maid, killed Sadyattes in his sleep. His reign had lasted for three years.

The next morning Gyges, quite at his ease, summoned both his friends and his enemies in the king's name, slew his adversaries and conciliated the rest with gifts. The people, however, made objection and the right of Gyges to the throne was formally referred to Delphi. The oracle supported Gyges but added that the Herakleidai would be given vengeance in the fifth generation.

Thus Gyges, son of Daskylos, became king of Lydia and took to wife the Mysian woman, cherishing no malice for all she had said against him to Sadyattes.

JUSTIN [i, 7]

The Lydians had many kings before Croesus, remarkable for various turns of fate; but none may be compared, in singularity of fortune, to Candaules. This prince used to speak of his wife, on whom he doted for her extreme beauty, to everybody, for he was not content with the quiet consciousness of his happiness, unless he also published the secrets of his married life; just as if silence concerning her beauty had been a detraction from it. At last to gain credit to his representations, he showed her undressed to his confidant, Gyges; an act by which he both rendered his friend, who was thus tempted to corrupt his wife, his enemy, and alienated his wife from him, by transferring, as it were, her love to another; for, soon after, the murder of Candaules was stipulated as the condition of her marriage with Gyges, and the wife, making her husband's blood her dowry, bestowed at once his kingdom and herself on her paramour.

PLATO [Republic ii, 14]

Gyges was a shepherd in the service of one who, in those days, was the king of Lydia. Owing to a great storm and also to an earthquake, the ground split open and a gap made its appearance near the place where he was watching his flocks. Amazed at the sight, Gyges went down into the cleft and, certainly according to the tale they tell, beheld marvels, among the rest a brazen horse, which was hollow and had doors. Gyges peeped in through them and saw a corpse inside, larger, as it appeared, than human size. There was nothing else at all but that. On its hand, however, was a ring of gold. This Gyges took off and came out. When the shepherds met as usual to make their monthly report to the king regarding his flocks, Gyges, who was wearing his ring, was one of the party. As he was sitting among the others he happened to turn the collet of it towards him and into the inside of his hand. The moment this was done he became invisible to those who sat near him, and they began to talk about him as they

would about one who was absent. Astonished, he ran his hand over
the ring, turned the setting out, and, as he did so, became visible again.
Upon observing the fact, he tested the ring to see whether it had this
power and found that such was really the case. Whenever he turned
the setting inward he disappeared; when he turned it outward he
became visible. Being now assured of the fact, he took measures to
become one of the messengers to the king. After his arrival he seduced
the queen, with her help set upon the king, slew him and took possession of the throne.

PHOTIUS

The wife of Candaules, whose name Herodotus does not mention,
was called Nysia. According to report, she possessed double pupils,
and was extremely sharp of sight, being in possession of the dragon
stone, and on this account perceived Gyges when he was passing out
of the door. Others call her Tudo, some Klytia, but Abas calls her
Habro. They say that Herodotus suppressed her name because his
favorite Plexiroos, a native of Halicarnassus, fell in love with a
courtezan by the name of Nysia, and failing to win her, hanged
himself in despair. For this reason Herodotus avoided mentioning
the name of Nysia because it was hateful to him.

PLUTARCH [*Greek Questions,* XLV]

Herakles, having slain Hippolyte and taken her axe with the rest
of her arms, gave it to Omphale. The kings of Lydia who succeeded
her carried this as one of their sacred insignia of office, and passed it
down from father to son until Candaules. Candaules, however, dis-
dained it and gave it to one of his companions to carry. When Gyges
rebelled and was making war upon Candaules, Arselis came with a
force from Mylasa to the assistance of Gyges, slew Candaules and his
companion, and took the axe to Caria with the other spoils of war.
And having set up a statue of Zeus, he put the axe in his hand and
called the god, Labrandeus, *labrys* being the Lydian word for the
Greek *pelekeus* (axe).

These differing accounts raise numerous questions: Can Herodotus
and Nicolaus both have derived their accounts from Xanthus? Did

Justin (Pompeius Trogus) borrow from Herodotus or from some other source? What is the significance of the stories told by Plato and Photius? Is Gyges an historical personage?

Part of the riddle was elucidated with great brilliance over half a century ago by Kirby Flower Smith in an article entitled, "The Tale of Gyges and the King of Lydia."[2] Professor Smith recognized the significance of the ring of Gyges, which made its wearer invisible, and the importance of the special vision of the queen (double pupil or dragon stone) which made it possible for her to see Gyges when his ring rendered him invisible to all others. The explanation is that we possess in these several accounts the fragments of a fairy tale. The following is an extract from Professor Smith's article:

> The character of all the incidents as well as of all the actors as they have gradually been revealed, points to one conclusion. So far as type is concerned, the legend of how Gyges became king of Lydia is the story of the Adventurer, the Giant, and the Princess, or in more general terms, of WIT, its contrasted Opponent and dupe, and its Reward . . . In this favorite combination of the fairy tale, the Adventurer, the Giant and Princess, no one was ever known to sympathize with the Giant . . . He is stupid and brutal and full of folly. The hero outwits him, the princess betrays him and both live happily ever after, on the fruits of their combined labors . . . Not only the character of Kandaules but his situation is the same. The possession of the Princess—usually a sorceress, as in this story—is the one real condition of his life and power. The kingdom is within her gift as a matter of course. . . .

> The Adventurer, like all successful adventurers, is usually remarkable for his address, versatility, and quickness of wit. His career is based upon the not over scrupulous use of these qualities and constitutes the real savor and lasting popularity of the story. That, in these respects, the legendary Gyges was a dignified prototype of Jack the Giant-killer and something very like a replica of Odysseus has become more and more evident as each detail of the popular story has come to light. . . .

> Gyges may win the confidence of Kandaules and become his

---

2. K. F. Smith, *The Tales of Gyges and the King of Lydia*, Baltimore 1902 (Reprinted from the *American Journal of Philology*, XXIII (1902).

trusted adviser but there is no friendship with the Giant-type. Kandaules lays bare the secret of his life and fortune. From that moment he is merely a pawn in the game. Gyges, the Odysseus, and Nysia, the Circe, of this story are now the principal characters. The scenes which follow—again suggestive, somehow, of the encounter of Odysseus and Circe—really constitute a duel of wits . . . But in the door episode ⟨Gyges⟩ tried his disappearing trick once too often. Without knowing it he now has to deal with a rival magician. His charm is met and detected by the counter-charm of Nysia. . . .

Gyges, first of the Lydian Mermnadae, rose to the throne in the seventh century B.C. His complex character, his commanding personality, his long and adventurous career, all united to make him a popular hero. He was also the first great barbarian with whom the Greeks had come in contact. It is evident that at an early date a mass of tradition had gathered about him . . . But of all the traditions regarding Gyges the most notable and dramatic was that which told how he became the king of Lydia. No less than five different versions of this event have reached us . . . There was, however, still another and far older version than any of these, though its age and ultimate source cannot be determined precisely. This was a genuine popular legend, a fairy-tale, describing the career of Gyges on his way to the throne. It probably originated among the Ionians and Lydians not far from the period of its hero. . . .

Gyges was conceived of as the favorite of Hermes and Aphrodite. The tradition of his beauty, strength and address, his versatility, cunning and energy, in short, of his likeness to Odysseus, goes back to the old popular story. The queen in that story had much in common with Circe. For the sake of greater clearness I append here a brief outline of my attempted reconstruction. The type is that of the Adventurer, Giant and Princess.

Gyges, the son of Daskylos and the ancestor of Croesus, was a shepherd when he was young in the service of Kanduales, king of Lydia. Once upon a time there was a storm and an earthquake so violent that the ground split open near the place where Gyges was watching his flocks. Gyges was amazed at the sight and finally went down into the cleft. The story tells of many wonderful things which he saw there (these details are lost).

Among these wonderful things was a brazen horse which was

hollow and had doors. In it was nothing but a corpse, of heroic size, and on one of its fingers was a gold ring.

Gyges took the ring and came out again.

Sometime later he attended the monthly assembly of the shepherds and while there accidentally discovered the qualities of his ring, as described by Plato. He then procured his appointment as one of the messengers to the king and went up to Sardis to seek his fortune.

After reaching Sardis an adventure with the ring brought him to the notice of Kandaules. At first, he was highly favored but later the king, who was cruel and whimsical, became suspicious of Gyges and set him at several tasks certain, as he supposed, to compass his destruction. Gyges, however, performed them all successfully with the aid of his ring, was reinstated in favor and given great estates.

Gyges was now not only rich and powerful but also admired and feared for his beauty, strength and address, and for his versatility and superhuman knowledge of what was going on. The king who, like everyone else, knew nothing of his ring, found Gyges invaluable, gave him the post of chief advisor and consulted him on all occasions.

There was one thing, however, which Kandaules had always kept jealously guarded, because it was the principal source, the real secret, of his power. This was his wife. She was a Mysian princess and exceedingly beautiful. But what made her indispensable to Kandaules was the fact that she was also very wise and powerful, being a mighty sorceress.

The one vulnerable spot in Kandaules was his passion for his wife. Like all who had ever seen her he was utterly bewitched by her beauty and as his confidence in Gyges increased he began to talk of it more and more freely. At last he insisted upon showing her. Gyges refused, forseeing mortal peril to himself from either, or both. But at last he was forced to comply and the programme devised by Kandaules was carried out as related by Herodotus.

Gyges gazed upon her. She was more lovely even than Kandaules had described her, and Gyges fell in love with her then and there. Finally, having turned his ring around to make himself invisible, Gyges left the room.

The queen, however, possessed a dragon-stone. Either when she first came into the room or as he was going out of it she had seen Gyges in spite of his magic ring. But she made no sign. She knew that the situation was due to Kandaules and swore to be avenged. When, therefore, Gyges, perhaps at her own instigation, came to her and declared his passion, revenge and, possibly, other considerations, prompted her to yield. Gyges was able to visit her unobserved on account of his magic ring and the intrigue went on for some time nothing being said on either side regarding the door episode.

At last, when the queen saw that Gyges was entirely in her power, and being also in love with him herself, she laid her plans and sent for him. When he arrived, she told him for the first time—as in Herodotus—that she had seen him passing out of the chamber, and why, that now Gyges must slay Kandaules or else die himself. Whatever the feelings of Gyges may have been, his situation, despite his magic ring, was even more desperate than in Herodotus. He had a sorceress to deal with and was committed to her by ties which he could not break, even if he so desired.

Gyges acceded, the destruction of Kandaules was planned and carried out by the two as described by Herodotus, and with the aid of the magic ring as hinted by Plato.

When the deed was accomplished she gave Gyges the kingdom, as she had promised. He made her his queen and they lived happily ever after.

Such is the tale of Gyges, ancestor of Croesus the Lydian and the founder of the house of the Mermnadai.

With Herodotus the old tale of Gyges emerges as a great tragedy of Destiny, a parallel, in prose, to the Agamemnon and the Oedipus Tyrannus. All the characters are worthy of the situation. No one can blame Kandaules for a madness which the gods have sent upon him and which drives him to his doom as inexorably as it raises Gyges to his high estate, each in his own despite. So, too, the irresponsible sorceress of the old fairy tale . . . becomes the evil genius of Kandaules. She vindicates her outraged womanhood. . . .

If the results of this article are justified by the testimony presented, they are worth consideration merely for the light which they throw upon the methods of Herodotus himself. One hardly knows which to esteem the more remarkable, his genius or his conservatism. The old tale of Gyges the Lydian was all but unchanged by him, yet under the spell of his surpassing art it rose once and for all to the beauty and dignity of a masterpiece.

So Professor Smith—and he was very close to the truth. He saw the elements of Greek tragedy in the Herodotus account, but we now have evidence suggesting that Herodotus did not make the dramatic refinements himself:

In 1949 a fragmentary Greek papyrus, dating from the second or third century A.D., was discovered which contained nearly fifty lines, or parts of lines, from a tragedy—probably of the first half of the fifth century B.C. and possibly by Phrynichus—which dealt with the story of Gyges, Kandaules, and the queen. In the surviving lines the queen relates that she saw Gyges in the room and thought at first that he had come to murder Kandaules. But then she realized that Kandaules was not asleep and must be partner to some deviltry. The next day the queen got Kandaules out of the palace before daybreak and sent for Gyges in order to demand an explanation. Perhaps the magic ring and the special vision of the queen are suggested by the queen's speech, "When I saw it was Gyges himself and not a ghost. . . ."

The play, therefore, and not Xanthus, was the source of Herodotus, and thus the divergence of the accounts of Herodotus and Nicolaus is explained.

The Historical Gyges

But Gyges *did* exist, and he *was* indeed the king of Lydia. This might be inferred from the testimony of Herodotus when he says, "Gyges, of whom Archilochus the Parian, who lived about the same time, made mention in a poem written in iambic trimeter verse." A line from this poem was later quoted by Plutarch, "I don't care for multimillioned Gyges . . ." Furthermore, the *Parian Marble*, a third century B.C. inscription from the island of Paros, gave the *floruit* of Archilochus as 682 B.C., and this would agree fairly well with the dates suggested by Herodotus' account. He gives the number of years for the reign of each of the Lydian kings from Croesus, who seems to have come to the throne about 560 B.C., back to Gyges. The latter, according to Herodotus, would have reigned from about 716–678 B.C. Roughly contemporary with Archilochus was another poet, Mimnermus of Colophon. According to Pausanias (second century A.D.), "Mimnermus wrote ⟨martial⟩ elegies for the wars of the people of Smyrna against Gyges and the Lydians."

The whole matter, however, was removed from the realm of inference in 1878 when Hormuzd Rassam, the friend and successor of Layard in charge of the excavations at Nineveh, found a great cuneiform cylinder which recorded the events of the first half of the reign of the great Assyrian king, Ashurbanipal (668–627 B.C.). The text of the Rassam Cylinder is as follows:

RASSAM CYLINDER [II, 95–125]

GU-UG-GU (Gyges), KING OF LU-UD-DI [Lydia], A REGION WHICH IS BY
THE SEA,

A FARAWAY PLACE, OF WHICH THE KINGS, MY FATHERS, HAD NOT HEARD ITS
NAME

MY IDENTITY IN A DREAM ASHUR, THE GOD, MY CREATOR, CAUSED TO BE
MADE KNOWN TO HIM,

SPEAKING THUS, "LAY HOLD OF THE FEET OF ASHURBANIPAL, KING OF
ASSYRIA AND

BY MEANS OF HIS NAME CONQUER YOUR ENEMIES."

THE DAY HE SAW THIS DREAM HE DESPATCHED HIS ENVOY

TO SALUTE ME. THIS DIVINE MESSAGE WHICH HE HAD WITNESSED

HE CONVEYED BY THE HANDS OF HIS MESSENGER AND REPEATED TO ME.

FROM THE VERY DAY ON WHICH HE LAID HOLD OF MY KINGLY FEET,

THE CIMMERIANS, WHO OPPRESSED THE PEOPLE OF HIS LAND,

WHO FEARED NOT MY FATHERS NOR YET GRASPED MY ROYAL FEET, HE
OVERCAME.

WITH THE HELP OF THE DEITIES ASHUR AND ISHTAR, MY SUPERIORS, FROM
AMONG THE LEADERS

OF THE CIMMERIANS WHOM HE HAD OVERCOME, TWO OFFICERS

IN BONDS, CHAINS OF IRON, HE CHAINED AND

CAUSED TO BE SENT TO ME ALONG WITH A SUITABLE PRESENT.

[Later] HIS ENVOY, WHOM HE HAD REGULARLY SENT TO SALUTE ME,

HE WITHDREW. INASMUCH AS THE WORD OF THE GOD ASHUR

HE DID NOT OBSERVE, HE TRUSTED IN HIS OWN POWER AND, PROUD OF
HEART,

HIS FORCES FOR AN ALLIANCE WITH TU-SHA-MI-IL-KI [Psammetichus],
   KING OF EGYPT,
WHO HAD CAST OFF THE YOKE OF MY SOVEREIGNTY, HE SENT. I MYSELF
   LEARNED THIS,
AND I PRAYED TO ASHUR AND ISHTAR: "TO HIS ENEMY MAY HIS CORPSE
   BE GIVEN AND
MAY THEY CARRY OFF HIS CARCASSE." JUST AS I PRAYED TO ASHUR, IT
   HAPPENED.
HIS CORPSE WAS GIVEN TO HIS ENEMIES, AND THEY CARRIED OFF HIS
   CARCASSE.
THE CIMMERIANS, WHOM HE HAD TRODDEN BENEATH HIS FEET BY VIRTUE
   OF MY NAME,
ATTACKED AND OVERCAME HIS WHOLE COUNTRY. HIS SUCCESSOR, HIS SON,
   SAT UPON HIS THRONE.
THE EVIL, WHICH BY THE RAISING OF MY HANDS, THE GODS, MY HELPERS
HAD VISITED UPON HIS FATHER, HE REPORTED THROUGH HIS MESSENGER AND
LAID HOLD OF MY KINGLY FEET, SAYING: "YOU ARE A KING WHOM THE
   GOD RECOGNIZES.
YOU CURSED MY FATHER AND EVIL BEFELL HIM.
I AM THE SLAVE WHO FEARS YOU. FAVOR ME AND LET ME BEAR YOUR YOKE."

The Rassam Cylinder proved the historicity of Gyges, but it raised new problems. Ashurbanipal did not begin to reign until 668, but, according to the chronology given by Herodotus, Gyges had died ten years earlier. On the other hand, Psammetichus, the first pharaoh of the Saite or Twenty-sixth Dynasty in Egypt, with whom Gyges made the alliance (according to Ashurbanipal) began to reign about 664 on the testimony of Herodotus himself. From what we know of Ashurbanipal's reign, the contacts with Gyges must have occurred in the period between 664 and 654. We shall return to this question after a consideration of the later history of Lydia.

The Later History of Lydia

HERODOTUS [1, 17 ff.]

Inheriting from his father a war with the Milesians, [Alyattes] pressed the siege against the city . . . In this way he carried on the war with the Milesians for eleven years . . . During six of these eleven years, Sadyattes, the son of Ardys, who first lighted the flames of this war, was king of Lydia, and made the incursions. Only the five following years belong to the reign of Alyattes, son of Sadyattes. . . .

[When Cyaxares was king of the Medes certain Scythians] fled to Alyattes in the guise of suppliants. Afterwards, on the refusal of Alyattes to give up his suppliants when Cyaxares sent to demand them of him, war broke out between the Lydians and the Medes, and continued for five years with various success. In the course of it the Medes gained many victories over the Lydians, and the Lydians also gained many victories over the Medes. Among their other battles was one night engagement. As, however, the balance had not inclined in favor of either nation, another combat took place in the sixth year, in the course of which, just as the battle was growing warm, day was on a sudden changed into night. This event had been foretold by Thales, the Milesian, who forewarned the Ionians of it, fixing the very year in which it took place. The Medes and Lydians, when they observed the change, ceased fighting, and were alike anxious to have terms of peace agreed on. Syennesis of Cilicia and Laby-netus of Babylon, were the persons who mediated between the parties, who hastened the taking of the oaths, and brought about the exchange of espousals. It was they who advised that Alyattes should give his daughter Aryenis in marriage to Astyages, the son of Cyaxares. . . .

⟨Having⟩ reigned over the land of Lydia for fifty-seven years, Alyattes died . . . On the death of Alyattes, Croesus, his son, who was thirty-five years old, succeeded to the throne. . . .

Croesus afterwards, in the course of many years, brought under his sway almost all the nations to the west of the Halys . . . When all these conquests had been added to the Lydian empire and the pros-perity of Sardis was now at its height, there came thither, one after another, all the sages of Greece living at the time, and among them, Solon, the Athenian. He was on his travels, having left Athens to be absent ten years, but really to avoid being forced to repeal any of the laws which, at the request of the Athenians, he had made for them . . . On this account, as well as to see the world, Solon set out upon his travels, in the course of which he went to Egypt to the court of Amasis, and also came on a visit to Croesus at Sardis.

Solon was archon at Athens in 594, the traditional date of his reform of the Athenian constitution. His travels would thus fall in 593–583, some 23 years before Croesus became king. Amasis, the great pharaoh of the Twenty-sixth Dynasty in Egypt, on Herodotus' own testimony reigned between 569 and 526. Thus, if Solon reformed the Athenian constitution in 594 and then went on his travels, he would have encountered neither Croesus nor Amasis. This is one of the many arguments for dating the reforms of Solon about 570 instead of 594. On the other hand, the encounter between Solon and Croesus as Herodotus describes it has all the marks of a folk tale. Plutarch in his Life of Solon followed the Herodotus story. Because his account is shorter than that of Herodotus, we shall use it here. Also Plutarch's comments on the chronological problem are interesting.

PLUTARCH [*Solon*]

That Solon should discourse with Croesus, some think not agreeable with chronology; but I cannot reject so famous and well-attested a narrative, and, what is more, so agreeable to Solon's temper, and so worthy of his wisdom and greatness of mind, because, forsooth, it does not agree with some chronological canons, which thousands have endeavored to regulate, and yet, to this day, could never bring their differing opinions to any agreement. . . .

Now when Solon came before him, and seemed not at all surprised [by Croesus' magnificence] nor gave Croesus those compliments he expected, but showed himself to all discerning eyes to be a man that despised the gaudiness and petty ostentation of it, he commanded them to open all his treasure houses, and carry him to see all his sumptuous furniture and luxuries, though he did not wish it; Solon could judge of him well enough by the first sight of him; and, when he returned from viewing all, Croesus asked him if he had ever known a happier man than he. And when Solon answered that he had known one Tellus, a fellow citizen of his own, and told him that this Tellus had been an honest man, had had good children, a competent estate, and died bravely in battle for his country, Croesus took him for an ill-bred fellow and a fool, for not measuring happiness by the abundance of gold and silver, and preferring the life and death of a private and mean man before so much power and empire. He

asked him, however, again, if, besides Tellus, he knew any other man
more happy. And Solon replying, "Yes, Cleobis and Biton, who were
loving brothers, and extremely dutiful sons to their mother, and,
when the oxen delayed her, harnessed themselves to the wagon, and
drew her to Hera's temple, her neighbors all calling her happy, and
she herself rejoicing; then, after sacrificing and feasting, they went to
rest, and never rose again, but died in the midst of their honor a
painless and tranquil death." "What," said Croesus angrily, "dost
not thou reckon us amongst the happy men at all?" Solon, unwilling
either to flatter or exasperate him more, replied, "The gods, O king,
have given the Greeks all other gifts in moderate degree; and so our
wisdom, too, is cheerful and homely, not a noble and kingly wisdom;
and this, observing the numerous misfortunes that attend all conditions,
forbids us to grow insolent upon our present enjoyment, or admire
any man's happiness that may yet, in the course of time, suffer change.
For the uncertain future has yet to come, with every possible variety
of fortune; and him only to whom the divinity has continued happiness unto the end we call happy; to salute as happy one that is still
in the midst of life and hazard, we think is little safe and conclusive as
to the crown and proclaim as victorious the wrestler that is still in
the ring." After this, he was dismissed, having given Croesus some
pain, but no instruction.

Subsequently, according to the legend, things went very badly for
Croesus. One of his sons was born deaf and dumb; the crown prince,
on whom he doted, was killed in a hunting accident. Then, Astyages,
king of Media and brother-in-law of Croesus, was overthrown by the
Persian revolution headed by Cyrus, said by Herodotus to be Astyages'
own grandson. The Herodotus story is more or less summarized by
Justin as follows:

JUSTIN [I, 4]

After several kings, the crown, by order of succession, descended to
Astyages. This prince, in a dream, saw a vine spring from the womb
of his only daughter, with the branches of which all Asia was over-
shadowed. The soothsayers being consulted concerning the vision,
replied, that he would have a grandson by that daughter, whose

greatness was foreshown, and the loss of Astyages' kingdom por-
tended. Alarmed at this answer, he gave his daughter in marriage, not
to an eminent man, nor to one of his own subjects ... but to Cambyses,
a man of mean fortune, and of the race of the Persians, which was at
that time obscure. But not having, even thus, got rid of his fear of
the dream, he sent for his daughter, while she was pregnant, that her
child might be put to death under the very eye of his grandfather.
The infant, as soon as it was born, was given to Harpagus, a friend of
the king's and in his secrets, to be killed. Harpagus fearing that if the
crown, on the death of the king, should devolve upon his daughter,
she might exact from the agent, for the murder of the child, that
revenge which she could not inflict on her father, gave the infant to
the herdsman of the king's cattle to be exposed. The herdsman, by
chance, had a son born at the same time: his wife, hearing of the
exposure of the royal infant, entreated, with the utmost earnestness,
that the child might be brought to her. The herdsman ... went back
into the wood, and found a dog by the infant, feeding it, and protect-
ing it from the beasts and birds of prey. [The baby was then adopted
by the herdsman's wife, and] the nurse had afterwards the name of
Spaco; for so the Persians call a dog.

In Herodotus the herdsman's child was stillborn, so that the exchange
of Cyrus and the dead child could be easily made. The herdsman's wife
was named "Spaco, which is in Greek Cyno, since in the Median tongue
the word *Spaca* means bitch."

We are rendered somewhat doubtful of the historicity of this story
about the birth of Cyrus the Great if we compare it with the tale of
Romulus and Remus.

LIVY [1, 3]

Amulius drove his brother out and ruled instead. Adding crime to
crime, he destroyed Numitor's male issue, and deprived his daughter
Rhea Silvia of the hope of children by the specious honor of appointing
her a Vestal, which obliged her to perpetual virginity. But . . . the
Vestal was ravished and produced twins ... The priestess was manacled
and thrown into prison, the boys he ordered thrown into the river.
Providentially, the Tiber had overflowed its banks into stagnant pools,
which made the regular channel inaccessible and led the messengers

to expect the infants to be drowned even in still water. So, as if discharging the king's orders fully, they set the boys down in the nearest overflow . . . The prevalent story is that, when the floating basket which carried the children was left on dry land by the receding water, a thirsty she-wolf from the nearby hills was attracted by the infants' wail and very tenderly gave them her teats; the keeper of the king's herd . . . found her licking the boys with her tongue. [He] carried them home to his wife Larentia to rear. Some hold that Larentia was called "She-wolf" by the shepherds. . . .

At any rate, Cyrus, like Romulus and Remus, was saved, grew to manhood and, also like Romulus and Remus, brought about the overthrow of the wicked king, his relative. Moreover, the story of Cyrus and the tale of Romulus and Remus call to mind two other rather similar accounts. The first is found in the cuneiform and relates to Sargon of Akkad (2350 B.C.); the second is taken from Josephus, the famous Jewish historian of the first century A.D.

THE BIRTH OF SARGON

I AM SARGON, MIGHTY KING, KING OF AKKAD

MY MOTHER WAS OF HUMBLE BIRTH; MY FATHER I DID NOT KNOW.

THE BROTHER OF MY FATHER DWELLS ON A MOUNTAIN.

MY CITY IS AZUPIRANU WHICH IS SITUATED ON THE BANK OF THE EUPHRATES.

MY MOTHER BORE ME AND BROUGHT ME FORTH IN SECRET.

SHE PLACED ME IN A BASKET OF REEDS: WITH PITCH THE OPENING SHE
    CLOSED;

SHE PUT ME INTO THE RIVER WHICH DID NOT ENGULF ME.

THE RIVER CARRIED ME TO AKKI, THE DIKE TENDER.

AKKI, THE DIKE TENDER, LIFTED ME UP . . .

AKKI, THE DIKE TENDER, RAISED ME AS HIS OWN SON.

. . . ⟨because⟩ ISHTAR LOVED ME . . . I CAME TO RULE THE KINGDOM.

JOSEPHUS [*Jewish Antiquities*, II, 9]

[For four hundred years the Jews labored for the Egyptians. Then,] one of those sacred scribes who were very sagacious in foretelling future events truly, told the king, that about this time there would be a child born to the Israelites who, if he were reared, would bring

the Egyptian dominion low . . . Which thing was so feared by the
king, that . . . he commanded that they should cast every male child
which was born to the Israelites into the river, and destroy it. . . .

A man whose name was Amram . . . was very uneasy about it,
his wife being then with child, and he knew not what to do . . .
Accordingly God had mercy on him, and was moved by his supplica-
tion. He stood by him in his sleep, and exhorted him not to despair
of his future favors. . . .

When the vision had informed him of these things, Amram
awakened and told it to Jochebed, who was his wife . . . [The child
was born]. They made an ark of bulrushes . . . daubed it over with
slime, which would naturally keep out the water from entering
between the bulrushes, and put the infant into it, and setting afloat
upon the river, they left its preservation to God; so the river received
the child, and carried him along. . . .

Thermouthis was the king's daughter. She was now diverting herself
by the banks of the river; and seeing a cradle borne along by the
current, she sent some that could swim, and bid them bring the cradle
to her. When . . . she saw the little child, she was greatly in love with
it . . . Thermouthis therefore perceiving him to be so remarkable a
child, adopted him for her son, having no child of her own. At one
time she carried Moses to her father. . . .

What Egyptian name for the princess Josephus had in mind is not
clear. It would indeed have been singular if the princess had been
named Thesmouthis rather than Thermouthis, for *thesm-t* in Egyptian
means female greyhound.

To come back to Croesus — when the Medes were overthrown by
the Persians under Cyrus, Croesus crossed the frontier into what had
been Median territory:

HERODOTUS [ι, 73 ff.]

There were two motives which led Croesus to attack Cappadocia:
firstly, he coveted the land, which he wished to add to his own
dominions; but the chief reason was, that he wanted to revenge on
Cyrus the wrongs of Astyages. . . .

(But Croesus was defeated, and Sardis was captured.)

With respect to Croesus himself, this is what befell him at the taking of the town. He had a son, of whom I made mention above, a worthy youth, whose only defect was that he was deaf and dumb. In the days of his prosperity Croesus had done the utmost that he could for him, and among other plans which he had devised, he had sent to Delphi to consult the oracle on his behalf [and was told that he would rue the day he first heard his son speak].

When the town was taken, one of the Persians was just going to kill Croesus, not knowing who he was. Croesus saw the man coming, but under the pressure of his affliction, did not care to avoid the blow, not minding whether or no he died beneath the stroke. Then this son of him, who was voiceless, beholding the Persian as he rushed toward Croesus, in the agony of his fear and grief burst into speech, and said, "Man, do not kill Croesus." This was the first time he had ever spoken a word, but afterwards he retained the power of speech for the remainder of his life.

Thus was Sardis taken by the Persians, and Croesus himself fell into their hands, after having reigned fourteen years . . . Then the Persians who had made Croesus prisoner brought him before Cyrus. Now a vast pile had been raised by his orders, and Croesus, laden with fetters, was placed upon it, and with him twice seven of the sons of the Lydians. I know not whether Cyrus was minded to make an offering of the first-fruits to some god or other, or whether he had vowed a vow and was performing it, or whether, as may well be, he had heard that Croesus was a holy man, and so wished to see if any of the heavenly powers would appear to save him from being burnt alive. However it might be, Cyrus was thus engaged, and Croesus was already on the pile, when it entered his mind in the depth of his woe that there was a divine warning in the words which had come from the lips of Solon, "No one while he lives is happy." When this thought smote him he fetched a long breath, and breaking his deep silence, groaned out aloud, thrice uttering the name of Solon. Cyrus caught the sounds, and bade the interpreters inquire of Croesus who it was he called on. They drew near and asked him, but he held his peace, and for a long time made no answer to their questionings, until at length, forced to say something, he exclaimed, "One I would give much to see converse with every monarch." Not knowing what he meant by this reply, the interpreters begged him to explain himself;

and as they pressed for an answer, and grew to be troublesome, he told them how, a long time before, Solon, an Athenian, had come and seen all his splendour, and made light of it; and how whatever he had said to him had fallen out exactly as he foreshowed, although it was nothing that especially concerned him, but applied to all mankind alike, and most to those who seemed to themselves happy. Meanwhile, as he spoke, the pile was lighted, and the outer portions began to blaze. Then Cyrus, hearing from the interpreters what Croesus had said, relented, bethinking himself that he too was a man, and that it was a fellow-man, and one who had once been as blessed by fortune as himself, that he was burning alive; afraid, moreover, of retribution, and full of the thought that whatever is human is insecure. So he bade them quench the blazing fire as quickly as they could, and take down Croesus and the other Lydians, which they tried to do, but the flames were not to be mastered.

Then, the Lydians say that Croesus, perceiving by the efforts made to quench the fire that Cyrus had relented, and seeing also that all was in vain, and that the men could not get the fire under, called with a loud voice upon the god Apollo, and prayed him, if he had ever received at his hands any acceptable gift, to come to his aid, and deliver him from his present danger. As thus with tears he besought the god, suddenly, though up to that time the sky had been clear and the day without a breath of wind, dark clouds gathered, and the storm burst over their heads with rain of such violence, that the flames were speedily extinguished. Cyrus, convinced by this that Croesus was a good man and a favorite of heaven [made him one of his advisors].

NICOLAUS OF DAMASCUS

Cyrus pitied Croesus, but the Persians were angry with him and raised a mighty funeral pyre at the foot of a lofty hill, from which they intended to behold the spectacle of his suffering. The royal train came forth from the palace gate and the king himself was in the midst, and all around strangers and citizens were flocking to see the sight. A little while and the officers appeared leading their prisoner in his chains, and with him twice seven Lydians; then there burst forth from the multitude of the city a piercing cry—men and women alike beating their breasts and weeping. The lamentation when the town was taken was not to be compared with this for bitterness . . . All this time Cyrus did not interfere, but let things take their course in hopes that some touch of compassion would move the hearts of the Persians. Now when Croesus came opposite the place where Cyrus sat, he cried to the king with a loud voice entreating to be allowed to see his son—it was his son who had been dumb and had recovered his speech whom he wished to see—who now spake readily and was a youth of sense and feeling.

[Croesus' son sought to cast himself upon the pyre, but was restrained. Croesus] the while sat upon the pyre, and with him the twice-seven Lydians, and the Persians with burning torches stood around and set the pyre alight. Then there was a silence, in the midst of which Croesus was heard to groan deeply and thrice utter the name of Solon. Cyrus wept at the sound, bethinking himself how greatly he was angering the gods by yielding to the will of the Persians, and burning a prince his equal in rank, and, once, in fortune. And now some of the Persians left Croesus and gathered around their king, and, seeing how sorrowful he was, entreated him to have the flames extinguished. So Cyrus sent his orders to put out the fire; but the pile was by this time in a blaze, and burnt so fiercely that no one could venture near to it. Then it is said that Croesus looked up to heaven and besought Apollo to come to his aid, since his very enemies were now willing to save him, but lacked the power. It was a gusty day, with a strong east wind blowing, but as yet there had been no rain. As Croesus prayed, the air grew suddenly dark, and clouds gathered together from all quarters, with much thunder and lightning, and such a storm of rain burst forth that, while it completely extinguished the blazing pyre, it almost drowned those who were seated thereon. [The Persians] . . . called loudly upon Cyrus to spare Croesus, and, prostrating themselves upon the ground, besought the gods to pardon them . . . Cyrus after this took Croesus to his palace and comforted him . . . In a little time the two princes became close friends, and Cyrus gave Croesus back his wives and children, and took him with him when he went away from Sardis. Some say that he would have been made governor of the place if he had not been fearful of his rebelling.

Of the Croesus story, the great translator of Herodotus, George Rawlinson, remarked:

The story of Croesus seems to have become to the romancers of the period what the old heroic tale of Oedipus was to the tragedians, the type of human instability. On the original historic facts were engrafted from time to time such incidents as the fancy of each writer deemed appropriate, and the whole gradually took the perfect form which delights us in Herodotus. The warning of Solon . . . the death of Atys [the crown prince], the profound grief of the father, the marvelous answers of the oracles, the recovery of speech by the dumb son, the scene upon the funeral pyre, the reproach addressed to Apollo—all these seem to be subsequent additions to the original historic outline, whereby it was filled up in accordance with the Greek conception of the fitness of things.

There was another version of the capture of Sardis and the behaviour of Croesus: that Croesus voluntarily prepared and ascended his own funeral pyre. It is found in the victory ode composed by Bacchylides (mid-fifth century B.C.) for Hiero of Syracuse. (The translation is adapted from that of E. Poste, *Bacchylides*, London 1898, pp. 32–33).

BACCHYLIDES

Once horse-taming Lydia's monarch, Croesus, was protected by golden-bowed Apollo when Sardis, doomed by Zeus, fell before the Persian host. When the grievous day arrived, the king would not await the added woe of a slave's all-tearful doom, but reared a pyre before the brazen walls of his palace court, and mounted thereon with his dear wife and fair-haired wildly weeping daughters. And raising his hands to high heaven, he cried in reproach: All-powerful spirit, where is the gratitude of the gods? Where is the King, Leto's son? . . .

So saying, he bade them kindle the pyre. His daughters shrieked and flung their hands about their mother's neck: for horrid to mortals is the face of imminent death. But when the fierce fire's gleam began to penetrate the pile, Zeus sent a black storm-cloud and quenched the yellow flame. Nothing is incredible that the divine will accomplishes. Then Delian-born Apollo bore off the old king to the land of the Hyperboreans . . . because of all mortals he had sent the richest offerings to holy Pytho [at Delphi].

Sardanapalus, the legendary last king of Assyria, whose name may represent a corruption of Ashurbanipal, had voluntarily met his fate in the same way as Croesus. This was the version given by Ctesias, the younger contemporary of Herodotus, who wrote a history of Persia. The Sardanapalus story is preserved for us in Diodorus Siculus and Athenaeus. Sardanapalus built a huge pyre, enclosed in which was a chamber of logs that contained his household and his treasures. So he perished in flames as the Medes under Cyaxares captured Nineveh.

In the more popular version of the story of Croesus, however, he became the trusted advisor of Cyrus and later accompanied Cyrus' son and successor, Cambyses, to Egypt.

HERODOTUS [III, 36]

Hereupon Croesus the Lydian thought it right to admonish Cambyses, which he did in these words following: "Oh! king, allow not thyself to give way entirely to thy youth, and the heat of thy temper, but check and control thyself . . . It is by thy father's wish that I offer thee advice; he charged me strictly to give thee such counsel as I might see to be most for thy good." In thus advising Cambyses, Croesus meant nothing but what was friendly. But Cambyses answered him, "Dost thou presume to offer me advice? Right well thou ruledst thy own country when thou wert a king, and right sage advice thou gavest my father Cyrus, bidding him cross the Araxes and fight the Massagetae in their own land, when they were willing to have passed over into ours. By thy misdirection of thine own affairs thou broughtest ruin upon thyself, and by thy bad counsel, which he followed thou broughtest ruin upon Cyrus, my father. But thou shalt not escape punishment now, for I have long been seeking to find some occasion against thee." As he thus spake, Cambyses took up his bow to shoot at Croesus; but Croesus ran hastily out, and escaped. So when Cambyses found that he could not kill him with his bow, he bade his servants seize him, and put him to death. The servants, however, who knew their master's humor, thought it best to hide Croesus; that so, if Cambyses relented, and asked for him, they might bring him out, and get a reward for having saved his life— if, on the other hand, he did not relent, or regret the loss, they might then despatch him. Not long afterwards, Cambyses did in fact regret the loss of Croesus, and the servants, perceiving it, let him know that he was still alive. "I am glad," said he, "that Croesus lives, but as for you who saved him, ye shall not escape my vengeance, but shall all of you be put to death." And he did even as he had said.

The story of the sage advisor who is sentenced to death, hidden away, and then restored to his position when the king regrets his anger was a great favorite in the Near East. The wise man, Ahiqar, advisor to Esarhaddon and then to his son, Sennacherib, had a somewhat similar experience and then was restored to power when war threatened between Assyria and Egypt. The Greeks transferred the Ahiqar story to the "biography" of Aesop, the supposed contemporary of Solon and Croesus, who was said to have been advisor to the king of Babylonia.

By this point it should be clear that the whole question of the sources of Herodotus for his history of Lydia and his use of these sources is complex and difficult. There are other matters which, if pertinent, would add to the complexity. Not the least of these is the fact that Ashurbanipal, whose connection with Sardanapalus and Gyges has already been mentioned, had a different "throne name" in Babylonia—it was Kandalanu!

IV

Criticism, External and Internal

ANYONE who has puzzled over a scribbled note with an illegible signature received in the mail, or cudgeled his brain over the possible use—or even the identity—of an unfamiliar object out of a Christmas package sent by a well-intentioned relative, will be in a position to appreciate a predicament frequently experienced by the researcher in ancient history. In archaeological work in the field, in museums, and even in the professor's office, documents and artifacts appear or are brought in which must be identified, and often authenticated, before they can be used as historical evidence. Forgeries, ancient and modern, are common enough and sometimes not easy to detect, but to place a genuine antiquity in its proper period and locality can pose difficulties, too. There is still some uncertainty about the famous Hermes and the infant Dionysus, a work of sculpture found over two generations ago at Olympia. It belongs to Greco-Roman antiquity, but is it the original work of Praxiteles, dedicated at Olympia, or is it a copy from the Roman period? The experts—on pottery, sculpture, or inscriptions, and the like—generally agree on matters of date and provenience, yet this is not always the case.

Fragments of inscriptions on stone, pieces of papyri, or pages from manuscripts can usually be dated on palaeographic grounds. Changes in letter forms and fashions in scribal hands are sufficiently well known at present so that even a novice, for example, can readily decide whether a papyrus dates from the Ptolemaic period, the principate, or the Byzantine era. At the end of the fifth century B.C., to cite another example, the Athenians officially abandoned their own epichoric alphabet for the Ionic. Again, the layman or general practitioner can guess with some certainty that an inscription from Athens may date from before or after that change, but an expert in epigraphy can narrow the margin considerably.

Nevertheless, it is one thing to arrive at an approximate date for a document or to say that it probably came from Athens or whatever place, yet it is another matter to make a more positive identification of its contents, particularly when it is fragmentary. One remembers the few Greek words on a scrap of papyrus found during the excavation of Dura-Europus on the Euphrates. A number of experts scratched their heads, but a great classical scholar, Levi Arnold Post, took one look at the papyrus and said, "Herodotus." He was right!

Sometimes the literary papyri from Egypt can be identified fairly quickly because they contain lines from known authors. Very often, however, a previously unknown work turns up; then, occasionally an attribution can be made on the basis of style and vocabulary. Medieval manuscripts containing theological material are frequently hard to identify, since many churchmen seem to have said about the same thing, and a great many of their effusions have survived.

The identification and authentication described above involves a process called *external criticism*. The main questions to be answered are: What is it? Where did it come from? What is its date? Is it genuine?

External criticism was called into play when the famous Dead Sea Scrolls were discovered in 1947. No one in modern times had ever seen biblical manuscripts of such antiquity. The scrolls were nearly a thousand years older than the earliest previously known Hebrew text of the Old Testament and five hundred years older than its oldest Greek manuscript, not counting materials found in the papyri. Many conservative scholars at first denied the genuineness of the scrolls or insisted that they must be dated in the second millennium A.D. Palaeographically, however, the script was related to that found on inscriptions of the first century B.C. and the first century of the Christian era. Secondly, the rolls were sealed in pottery jars which could be dated to that same period, and among the artifacts found in the caves where the writings had been secreted were coins, no one of which was later than the first century A.D. A Carbon-14 analysis of the linen in which the scrolls were wrapped gave an age of 1917 years, plus or minus 200; in short, the linen could be as old as the second century B.C. or as recent as the second century A.D. Furthermore, from both the third and the eighth centuries A.D. there were accounts of such writings having been found in jars in the caves of the Dead Sea area. The Dead Sea Scrolls therefore were genuine; they were not modern forgeries, nor were they of medieval date.

Recently, a somewhat more difficult problem was posed by the discovery of a Greek inscription which seemed to relate to events in the fifth century B.C. It had to do, in fact, with the Persian invasion of Greece in 480 B.C. when Xerxes led a great army and fleet along the north Aegean coast and down into Greece. At Thermopylae the Spartan king, Leonidas, was to hold back the Persians in the narrow pass while the Greek fleet occupied the strait at Artemisium to prevent the Persian navy from turning the Greek land position as they had already done at Tempe farther north. The most important literary accounts were the following:

HERODOTUS [VIII, 1–2]

The Greeks engaged in the sea-service [at Artemisium] were the following. The Athenians furnished a hundred and twenty-seven vessels to the fleet, which was manned in part by the Plataeans, who, though unskilled in such matters, were led by their active and daring spirit to undertake this duty; the Corinthians furnished a contingent of forty vessels; the Megarians sent twenty; the Chalcidians also manned twenty, which had been furnished to them by the Athenians; the Aeginetans came with eighteen; the Sicyonians with twelve; the Lacedaemonians with ten; the Epidaurians with eight; the Troezenians with five; the Styreans with two; and the Ceans with two triremes and two penteconters. Last of all, the Locrians of Opus came in aid with a squadron of seven penteconters.

Such were the nations which furnished vessels to the fleet now at

Artemisium; and in mentioning them I have given the numbers of ships furnished by each. The total number of ships thus brought together was two hundred and seventy-one. . . .

(The Persians then sent 200 ships to sail around Euboea and come up behind the Greeks. When these ships were in position, the Persians planned to attack both the front and rear of the Greeks. But the fleet sent around Euboea was damaged by a storm, and 53 ships came from Attica to Artemisium to reinforce the Greeks and bear the news of the disaster to the Persian ships. Herodotus had already numbered the total Athenian fleet at 200; these 53 new ships plus the 127 manned by Athenians and Plataeans and 20 by the Chalcidians would give the total of 200. After a sea battle at Artemisium, the Greek fleet withdrew to Salamis when the fall of Thermopylae occurred.)

HERODOTUS [VIII, 40 ff.]

Meanwhile, the Grecian fleet, which had left Artemisium, proceeded to Salamis, at the request of the Athenians, and there cast anchor. The Athenians had begged them to take up this position, in order that they might convey their women and children out of Attica. . . .

So while the rest of the fleet lay to off this island, the Athenians cast anchor along their own coast. Immediately upon their arrival, proclamation was made, that every Athenian should save his children and household as best he could; whereupon some sent their families to Aegina, some to Salamis, but the greater number to Troezen. . . .

PLUTARCH [Life of Themistocles]

At length his [Themistocles'] opinion prevailed, and he obtained a decree that the city should be committed to the protection of Athena, Queen of Athens; that they who were of age to bear arms should embark, and that each should see to sending away his children, women, and slaves where he could. This decree being confirmed, most of the Athenians removed their parents, wives, and children to Troezen. . . .

HERODOTUS [VIII, 44 ff.]

[In addition to the Peloponnesian vessels,] from the mainland of Greece beyond the Peloponnese, came the Athenians with a hundred and eighty ships, a greater number than that furnished by any other people; and these were now manned wholly by themselves; for the Plataeans did not serve aboard the Athenian ships at Salamis. . . .

The [Persians found Athens] forsaken; a few people only remained in the temple [of Athena on the Acropolis], either keepers of the treasure, or men of the poorer sort. These persons having fortified the Acropolis with planks and boards, held out against the enemy . . . [but were slain].

CORNELIUS NEPOS [*Themistocles*, II–IV]

When the news of his [Xerxes'] approach was spread through Greece, and the Athenians, on account of the battle of Marathon, were said to be the chief objects of his attack, they sent to Delphi to ask what they should do in their present circumstances. As soon as they put the question, the Pythian priestess replied that "they must defend themselves with wooden walls." As no one understood to what this answer tended, Themistocles suggested that it was Apollo's recommendation that they should put themselves and their property on board their ships, for that such were the wooden walls intended by the god. This plan being approved, they added to their former vessels as many more with three banks of oars, and carried off all their goods that could be moved, partly to Salamis and partly to Troezen. The citadel, and sacred things, they committed to the priests, and a few old men, to be taken care of; the rest of the town they abandoned.

This measure of Themistocles was unsatisfactory to most of the states, and they preferred to fight on land. A select force was accordingly sent with Leonidas, king of the Lacedaemonians, to secure the pass of Thermopylae, and prevent the barbarians from advancing further. This body could not withstand the force of the enemy, and were all slain on the spot. But the combined fleet of Greece, consisting of three hundred ships, of which two hundred belonged to the Athenians, engaged the king's fleet for the first time at Artemisium, between Euboea and the mainland; for Themistocles had betaken himself to the straits, that he might not be surrounded by numbers. Though they came off here with success equally balanced, yet they did not dare to remain in the same place, because there was apprehension, lest, if part of the enemy's fleet should get round Euboea, they should be assailed by danger on both sides. Hence it came to pass that they left Artemisum, and drew up their fleet on the coast of Salamis, over against Athens.

Xerxes, having forced a passage through Thermopylae marched at once to the city, and as none defended it, destroyed it by fire, putting to death the priests that he found in the citadel. . . .

Such were the accounts given by the literary sources of the events leading up to the Battle of Salamis. In 1959, however, M. H. Jameson of the University of Pennsylvania, found among other antiquities collected in a coffeehouse in Troizen the following text inscribed on a stone tablet:[1]

Be it resolved by the Council [of the 500] and the People [assembly]. Themistocles, son of Neocles, of the deme of Phrearri, moved: to entrust the city to Athena, Queen of Athens, and to all the other gods to guard and protect from the barbarian . . . The Athenians and the foreigners who live in Athens are to evacuate the women and children to Troezen . . . The old men and possessions that are moveable are to be taken to Salamis. The treasurers and the priestesses are to stay on the Acropolis and guard the possessions of the gods. All other Athenians and the foreigners liable to military service are to go aboard the 200 ships that are prepared and oppose the barbarian . . . along with the Spartans, Corinthians, the Aeginetans. . . .

(Several lines deal with the appointment by the generals of the commanders of the 200 ships and the apportionment of the crews.)

When the ships have been manned, 100 of them are to engage the enemy at Artemisium in Euboea, and the other 100 are to be stationed off Salamis and the coast of Attica. . . .

The beginning of the decree is very reminiscent of Plutarch's account, but the bulk of it is certainly not in accord with Herodotus' story. For one thing, Herodotus placed the abandonment of Athens *after* Thermopylae and Artemisium, while the inscription dated it *before* these events. True, the inscription and Nepos are in accord on this point, but Nepos, an embryonic Latin biographer of the first century B.C., could hardly

---

1. For an account and photograph of this inscription, see M. F. Jameson, "How Themistocles Planned the Battle of Salamis," *Scientific American*, 204 (March 1961), pp. 111–120.

be claimed to have first hand information. What was the explanation?

First of all, this purported Athenian decree had been found in Troizen, not in Athens. Secondly, its opening formula was not that of a fifth-century Athenian decree but of the late fourth century or after. A careful analysis of the stone itself and the palaeography of the inscription was made by experts in epigraphy who generally agreed that the inscription had been made at Troizen by a native stone cutter in the third century B.C., two hundred years after the decree was supposed to have been promulgated.

This document, then, was not a copy of an actual decree of 480 B.C. It might be a paraphrase. On the other hand, several fourth-century forgeries of purported fifth-century documents were already known, including an oath supposed to have been sworn by the Greeks before the Battle of Plataea in 479.

Scholarly opinion has been divided on the question of paraphrase or forgery, but it is safe to assume that the final verdict will be that this document, though a genuine text of the third century, is historically valuable for what it tells us about political propaganda in that period rather than as having a bearing on the events before the Battle of Salamis in 480.

Internal Criticism

While "external criticism" is ordinarily concerned with establishing the identity of a document or an artifact and determining whether it is authentic or spurious, "internal criticism" is applied to evaluate the evidence of sources of which the identity is known. A perfectly genuine document may be of little or no value for a variety of reasons: its author may have been a mere plagiarist, incurably biassed, lacking in perception, or just a plain liar. The question which internal criticism seeks to answer then is: "What is it worth?"

Getting at the truth is not only an historical problem, but it is also one encountered in day-to-day living. Two automobiles collide at an intersection. Each driver may insist that it was the other man's fault, and a half dozen witnesses may very well give six different versions of the accident. Several months later when the case is tried in court, the incident may be quite hazy in the minds of those called to testify. It is reasonably certain, however, that no outsider, who just happened to hear the story from some one else, will be asked to confirm the testimony of an eyewitness.

In the "Tale of Gyges" we have already seen an example of internal criticism. This was a typical problem of its kind, but other and quite different situations arise in which sources must be evaluated. We may lead up to a common type of problem by first considering another matter:

If, for example, we intend to use one of the ancient authors as a source, we must first make sure that we have a reliable text. We do not possess the original manuscript written or dictated by Thucydides—or any other ancient author, for that matter. The extant manuscripts are *copies of copies* many times removed from the originals. It is no easy thing to make a perfect copy, and the scribes of antiquity and the middle ages rarely succeeded in doing so. What usually happened was that if two scribes each made a copy of the same manuscript, each man introduced his own set of errors in spelling, omission of words and even lines, interpolations, and the like. The next scribe who copied the manuscript of Scribe A would perpetuate his mistakes and add some new ones of his own; likewise, the scribe who copied the manuscript of Scribe B would produce a text that resembled that of Scribe B, rather than that of Scribe A, along with some new and unique errors. Thus, in order to procure a reliable text of an ancient author the extant manuscripts must be collated (compared) and a great effort made to reconstruct the original text.

The process may be illustrated by a simple hypothetical example:

Let us suppose that we are concerned with an author known to have written before the tenth century A.D. We possess several manuscripts of the fourteenth and fifteenth centuries in which a certain line is consistently rendered: "The queen was in the parlor eating bread and honey." In our earliest extant manuscript, dated in the twelfth century, the page is torn so that all that remains is "The queen was in the parlor eating . . ." In addition, there are five other manuscripts of the thirteenth and fourteenth centuries which present variant readings as follows:

A. (*13th cent.*) The queen was in her parlor eting bread and honey.
B. (*13th cent.*) The queen was in the parlor eating bread and milk.
C. (*14th cent.*) The queen was in her parlor eting bread and honey.
D. (*14th cent.*) The queen was in the parlour eating bread and milk.
E. (*14th cent.*) The queen was in her parlour eting honey.

We may therefore conclude that the correct reading is "The queen was in the parlor eating bread and honey" and that the early twelfth-century manuscript, when whole, contained this reading. Furthermore, this same twelfth-century manuscript may have been the archetype (source) from which the other manuscripts, with the exception of C, D, and E, were derived. The probable relationships of the manuscripts are shown in the diagram below.

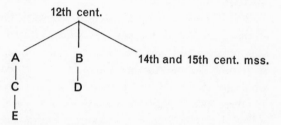

Turning from manuscripts to the ancient authors, it may be noted that out and out plagiarism was common, especially in the later years of the Roman Empire and on through the succeeding periods. The late Roman, Byzantine, and medieval writers often copied passages word for word from their predecessors without any acknowledgement. No knowledge of Latin is required to detect a certain lack of originality in the following passages.

Eutropius (c. 369 A.D.)
Cochen et Ctesiphontem, urbes nobilissimas, cepit.
Et cum castra supra Tigridem haberet, vi divini fulminis periit.

Festus (c. 369 A.D.)
Cochen et Ctesiphontem, urbes nobilissimas, cepit.
Quem victor istius gentis super Tigridem haberet, fulminis ictu interiit.

Epitome de Caesaribus (395)
Hic apud Ctesiphonta ictu fulminis interiit.

St. Jerome (c. 395)
Cochem et Ctesiphontem, nobilissimas hostium urbes cepisset, super Tigridem castra ponens fulmini ictus interiit.

On the basis of this evidence alone, it would not be possible to decide whether Eutropius copied from Festus, or Festus from Eutropius, or whether they (as well as the other two authors) drew upon a common source not now extant. The essential point is that, although the four authors tell the same story, it is no more credible than if only one of them had told it. Furthermore, it would be pointless to list as 'sources' later writers who repeat verbatim the accounts of Festus or Eutropius.

On the other hand, when discrepancies occur in the accounts of authors who customarily subscribe to the same tradition, it is often possible to reconcile the variant accounts by discovering the manuscript errors or misunderstandings which gave rise to the differences. The process will be much the same as that used above in establishing the correct reading of a text.

The Roman emperor Carus (A.D. 282–283), the same man described in the preceding Latin passages who captured the Persian cities in Mesopotamia and was then struck by lightning, is said by Eutropius, St. Jerome, Sextus Aurelius Victor (A.D. 360), Syncellos (ninth century A.D.), and Zonaras (twelfth century) to have been born in Gaul. The first three specify Narbo in Gaul as his birthplace, and this is confirmed independently in a poem by Sidonius, a fifth-century native of Narbo.

This apparent unanimity of opinion, however, is marred by two variants. The author of the *Vita Cari*, one of a series of imperial biographies known as the Augustan History and dating probably from about A.D. 360, says that Carus was born in Illyricum, or possibly in Rome or Milan. Moreover, the *Epitome de Caesaribus* puts the birthplace of Carus in Narbona, an unknown town.

Joseph Justus Scaliger, a brilliant scholar of the sixteenth century, was inclined to accept the testimony of the *Vita Cari* that Carus was born in Illyricum, especially after he discovered that Narbona was a variant spelling for Narona, a town in Dalmatia, a possible subdistrict of Illyricum. Scaliger's theory, however, is somewhat weakened by the fact that we now know the Augustan History to be generally unreliable, and his position becomes untenable when the *Epitome de Caesaribus* is subjected to closer scrutiny.

In the first place, the *Epitome* is ordinarily presumed to be a condensation of the earlier *De Caesaribus* of Sextus Aurelius Victor. The text of the *De Caesaribus* reads "Narbone patria" which clearly indicates Narbo as the birthplace of Carus, but even more positive evidence can be obtained from a comparison of the texts of the *Epitome* and Eutropius:

Epitome	*Eutropius*
Carus, Narbonae natus, imperavit annos duos. Iste confestim Carinum et Numerianum Caesares fecit.	Carus. . . . Narbone natus in Gallia. Is confestim Carinum et Numerianum filios Caesares fecit.

The *Epitome* exists in a single manuscript, while there are many manuscripts of Eutropius. "Narbonae natus," born in Narbona, must be a scribal error for "Narbone natus," born in Narbo.

From this relatively simple problem we may go on to one somewhat more complex that involves, nevertheless, the same group of ancient authors.

After the death of Carus in December 283, the Persian war was terminated, and Numerian, the son of Carus, led the Roman army back into Roman territory. Edward Gibbon reconstructed subsequent events as follows:

> But the talents of Numerian were rather of the contemplative rather than of the active kind. When his father's elevation reluctantly forced him from the shade of retirement, neither his temper nor his pursuits had qualified him for the command of armies. His constitution was destroyed by the hardships of the Persian war; and he had contracted, from the heat of the climate, such a weakness in his eyes, as obliged him, in the course of a long retreat, to confine himself to the solitude and darkness of a tent or litter. The administration of all affairs, civil as well as military, was devolved on Arrius Aper, the Praetorian Prefect, who, to the power of his important office, added the honor of being the father-in-law to Numerian. The imperial pavilion was strictly guarded by his most trusty adherents; and during many days Aper delivered to the army the supposed mandates of their invisible sovereign.

> It was not till eight months after the death of Carus that the Roman army, returning by slow marches from the banks of the Tigris, arrived on those of the Thracian Bosphorus. The legions halted at Chalcedon in Asia, while the court passed over to Heraclea, on the European side of the Propontis. But a report soon circulated through the camp, at first in secret whispers, and at length in loud clamours,

of the emperor's death, and of the presumption of his ambitious minister, who still exercised the sovereign power in the name of a prince who was no more. The impatience of the soldiers could not long support a state of suspense. With rude curiosity they broke into the imperial tent, and discovered only the corpse of Numerian. The gradual decline of his health might have induced them to believe that his death was natural; but the concealment was interpreted as an evidence of guilt, and the measures which Aper had taken to secure his election became the immediate occasion of his ruin. Yet, even in the transport of their rage and grief, the troops observed a regular proceeding, which proves how firmly discipline had been re-established by the martial successors of Gallienus. A general assembly of the army was appointed to be held at Chalcedon, whither Aper was transported in chains, as a prisoner and a criminal. A vacant tribunal was erected in the midst of the camp, and the generals and tribunes formed a great military council. They soon announced to the multitude that their choice had fallen upon Diocletian, commander of the domestics or bodyguards, as the person most capable of revenging and succeeding their beloved emperor. The future fortunes of the candidate depended on the chance or conduct of the present hour. Conscious that the station which he had filled had exposed him to some suspicions, Diocletian ascended the tribunal, and, raising his eyes towards the Sun, made a solemn profession of his own innocence, in the presence of that all-seeing Deity. Then, assuming the tone of a sovereign and a judge, he commanded that Aper should be brought in chains to the foot of the tribunal. "This man," said he, "is the murderer of Numerian;" and without giving him time to enter on a dangerous justification, drew his sword, and buried it in the breast of the unfortunate prefect. A charge supported by such decisive proof was admitted without contradiction, and the legions, with repeated acclamations, acknowledged the justice and authority of the emperor Diocletian.

Gibbon's account represents an attempt to utilize all the material contained in the sources. He used the *Vita Cari*, Eutropius, Sextus Aurelius Victor, the *Epitome de Caesaribus*, St. Jerome, Zonaras, and a seventh century work in Greek known as the Paschal Chronicle. All agree that Numerian was killed by Aper, the praetorian prefect. With the exception of the *Epitome* and the Paschal Chronicle, all agree that a trial was held at which Diocletian accused Aper of the murder and despatched him with a sword. Victor adds that Diocletian swore by the sun god that he himself was innocent of Numerian's death, while the *Vita Cari* notes "When someone inquired how Numerian had been killed, he [Diocletian] drew his sword and, pointing toward Aper, ran him through, adding these words: 'This is the author of the death of Numerian!'" Zonaras says that when the investigation was held by the soldiers concerning the death of Numerian, Diocletian pointed to Aper and said, "This man is his murderer." Then he pierced him with his sword. The Paschal Chronicle merely says that the murder of Numerian was discovered in Perinthus (Heraclea) in Thrace; the acclamation of Diocletian by the soldiers in Chalcedon; and the ceremonies of his accession in Nicomedia. John of Antioch, only fragments of whose work survive, also places the accession ceremonies in Nicomedia, but the details regarding Perinthus and Chalcedon are found only in the Paschal Chronicle.

Now, the ultimate source of most of the Paschal Chronicle is known to have been the *Chronicle* of Eusebius of Caesarea, a prominent Christian scholar of the early fourth century A.D. The *Chronicle* of Eusebius is no longer extant, but it was translated into Latin by St. Jerome, passages from the *Chronicle* can be recognized in the Byzantine writers, and Armenian and Syriac versions of the work also exist. St. Jerome says nothing about Perinthus or Thrace or Chalcedon; rather, his account is very close to that of the other fourth-century Latin writers:

St. Jerome. "Numerianus cum ob oculorum dolorum lecticula veheretur insidiis Apri soceri sui occisus est. . . ."

Eutropius. "Numerianus . . . cum oculorum dolore correptus in lecticula veheretur, impulsore Apro, qui socer eius erat, per insidias occisus est."

Victor. "Numerianus . . . Apri praefecti praetorio soceri insidiis extinguitur."

Epitome. "Numerianus . . . cum oculorum dolore correptus in lecticula veheretur, impulsore Apro, qui socer eius erat, per insidias occisus est."

Vita Cari. "[Numerianus] cum oculos dolore coepisset . . . ac lectica portaretur, factione Apri soceri sui . . . occisus est."

On the other hand, the Armenian and Syriac versions of Eusebius,

both dating from the fifth century A.D., make a simple statement that
Numerian was killed in Thrace; this is also found in the Armenian
historian, Moses of Khorene. All this can be explained by a closer
examination of the text of the Paschal Chronicle. A literal translation
of the Greek is as follows:

"Then killed was Numerian in Perinthus of Thrace, now called
Heraclea, by Aper, the praetorian prefect."

But St. Jerome, supposedly also translating Eusebius, merely has:
"Numerian . . . by Aper, his father-in-law (*socer*) was killed."

Victor adds that Aper was the praetorian prefect and father-in-law
of Numerian. Syncellos (ninth century), like St. Jerome indebted to
Eusebius, says that Numerian was killed by his own father-in-law, and
Zonaras (twelfth century) has "father-in-law and praetorian prefect."
For the Latin word *socer* (father-in-law), Syncellos and Zonaras, writing
in Greek, use the Greek equivalent, *pentheros*.

Pentheros is the clue. The Armenian and Syriac authors were fre-
quently confused by unfamiliar words which they found in their Greek
sources. In writing about Carus, the father of Numerian, Moses of
Khorene misunderstood the statement of the Greek that Carus was killed
by a thunderbolt (*keraunos*). The Greek (*en kerauno*) was rendered as *in
Yrhinon* (a place name), and the story was also given another twist as
Moses made *Keraunos* into Gornag, a personal name. The general,
Gornag, was then said to have defeated Carinus, the son of Carus.

This, then, is what happened:

A Greek original, possibly Eusebius, read "Then killed was Numerian
by his father-in-law (pentheros), Aper, the praetorian prefect." A non-
Greek scribe, translating into Armenian, wrote, "Then killed was
Numerian in Perinthus by Aper, his praetorian prefect." But Perinthus
no longer existed; its name had been changed to Heraclea. So the scribe,
or the next copyist, added "Perinthus in Thrace, now called Heraclea."
The Paschal Chronicle, which used (among others) an Armenian source
also employed by Moses of Khorene, then translated the Armenian
back into Greek.

And from this, it is clear that we cannot subscribe to Gibbon's
reconstruction in every detail.[2]

2. The material on Carus and his sons is based on two articles by T. Jones: "A Note
on Marcus Aurelius Carus," *Classical Philology*, XXXVII (1942), pp. 193–194 and "The
Death of Numerian and the Accession of Diocletian," *Ibid.*, XXXV (1940), pp. 302–303.

V

The Labyrinth of Chronos

OCCASIONALLY it is said that our calendar is imperfect and needs reform. In the fifty-one years beginning with 1950 and including A.D. 2000, New Year's Day has fallen, or will fall, eight times on Sunday, eight on Friday, and seven times on each of the other days of the week. Consequently, the working man, or woman, will lose fifteen holidays (or thirty counting Christmas). On the other hand, there will be fifteen long week-ends when New Year's Day falls on Friday or Monday. This means the loss of fifteen working days with a resultant setback for our national production although this will be somewhat tempered by the increased business of morticians and the manufacturers of aspirin and tomato juice.

The Congress of the United States, or at least part of it, has viewed with alarm the fact that the first half of our year (January–June) is normally three days shorter than the second half. It has been proposed that we should reconstitute our months so that each quarter of the year will consist of ninety-one days—two months of thirty days, and one of thirty-one. The last, the 365th, day of the year will not belong to any month but will be called New Year's Day or Old Year's Day, or something of the kind. June will normally have thirty-one days, except on leap years when there will be an extra or Leap Year Day. What unique distinction awaits the first child to be born on June 32!

It has long been urged by a minute, but well-organized, minority that we should discard our old months and create thirteen new ones each twenty-eight days in length. If New Year's Day and Leap Year Day were not attached to any month, then each of the new months could begin on Sunday and end on Saturday. Thus, for example, the second, ninth, sixteenth, and twenty-third of any month would always be a Monday. This would be very tidy—and monotonous in the extreme. Thanksgiving, Easter, and Mother's Day would not be greatly affected by such changes, but the situation of Christmas and Independence Day might be a little uncertain. And what would we call the thirteenth month?

Perhaps we should not worry about finding an appropriate name for a hypothetical thirteenth month when we have already accepted without much question for the last 2000 years a *twelfth* month named DECEMBER. We also have a week in which the days have such curious names as Sun-day, Moon-day, Saturn-day—and Woton's-day, Thor's-day, and so forth. And what of the present era? Anno Domini 1966 is commemorative of an individual who was born, as most people believe, 1970 years previously—in 4 B.C.!

In short, our present calendrical and associated practices have been snatched from a cultural grab bag, and it is quite impossible to reconcile them completely. Long ago the year, the month, and the week were separate entities which people did not try very hard to synchronize. The year, of course, is the solar year, a period of roughly $365\frac{1}{4}$ days required for the earth to complete its circuit around the sun. The month (moon-th) had its beginning with the lunar month, the time between the appearance of successive new moons which averages twenty-nine and a half days. The week came into general use rather late, and it was not always or everywhere a seven-day period. The origins of the week are obscure, but the seven-day week seems to have been related to the phases of the moon: the new, the half, the full, and the old moon. These, of course, are quite regular in their succession. For example, in March 1965 the four phases could be observed on the third, tenth, seventeenth, and twenty-fourth respectively; the new moon then appeared eight days later on April 1, and the April sequence went 1, 8, 15, and 23.

How did people first measure the passage of time? The day and the lunar month (with its varying twenty-nine and thirty day lengths) were easy and convenient ways of reckoning. Then, there was the repetitive cycle of the seasons which gave a rough approximation of the solar year. In Hesiod's *Works and Days* the various divisions of the farmer's year are related to astronomical phenomena. The (morning) setting of the Pleiades (November) signals the time for ploughing, and their rising in May heralds the harvest period (lines 383–386). The evening rising of Arcturus (February) warns the farmer that he should prune his grapevines (564–570). He must winnow his grain when Orion appears at dawn (July), while the morning rising of Arcturus (September) tells him that the grape harvest is nigh (609–611). But when the Pleiades and Orion begin to set, it is time to plough once more, "and so the completed year will fitly pass beneath the earth (617)."

In Egypt the dawn rising of Sirius was observed to coincide with the beginning of the summer solstice and the annual Nile flood. For all practical purposes the period between these successive heliacal risings of Sirius is identical with the solar year; the variation is just under nineteen hours a century. Consequently, the Egyptians were provided with data which made it easy for them to approximate the length of the solar year, but it was many centuries before other nations shared this knowledge. The Sumerians used a lunar month, and a cycle of twelve such months constituted their year which fell short of the solar year by ten or twelve days. They compensated for this by adding a thirteenth month on an average of once every three years, and it was not apparently until the Neo-Babylonian period that the Mesopotamians discovered that 235 lunations (lunar months) equal 19 solar years. The Sumerian months were named for seasonal activities and festivals: at Drehem, for example, the first month was the Month of Eating Gazelles, and the twelfth was the Harvest Month.

The Romans had a rather imperfect calendar until it was revised by Julius Caesar, with the assistance of Greek astronomers, in 45 B.C. His Julian calendar was used in western Europe for sixteen centuries, but it had the defect of inserting too many leap years with the result that nearly one day was lost in every hundred years. It is well known that the British did not adopt the improved calendar of Pope Gregory XIII (1582) until 170 years later than its introduction on the continent so that poor George Washington was born on February 11 (Julian) instead of February 22 (Gregorian).

Nevertheless, no matter how vaguely it might be defined, the year became the common unit of time reckoning. Within this framework, however, there was a great deal of variation. There was no uniformity about the beginning of the year: the people of the Near East tended to favor either the spring, right after the grain harvest, or the autumn, when the fall rains came and the planting occurred. In Athens the year began in July; in Rome, on the first of January. There were also several methods of designating or distinguishing each year, and various eras were employed for reckoning larger chunks of time.

A common system was that of the *regnal* year: "the first year of King *X*; the second year of King *X*, etc." This was used in Judah and Israel, and it was also used by the Neo-Babylonians, the Romans of the imperial period, and by many others. In the Ur III and Old Babylonian periods, for example, *year formulae* were employed: "the year when so and so became king; the year when such and such a town was destroyed; the year when such and such a canal was built." Until a year was named, sometimes several months after it had begun, it was called the year *after* the preceding one: if the preceding year was "the year when *X* became king," the next year, until named, would be "the year after *X* became king." Then, there was the custom of naming the year after certain magistrates (eponymous officials). At Athens people spoke of "the year in which so and so was archon;" at Rome, "the year when *X* and *Y* were consuls." Eponymous also were the *limmu* officials of Assyria.

With regard to the era system, the Romans, for example, counted so many years *ab urbe condita*, from the supposed founding of Rome in 753 B.C. In the Jewish reckoning, the year 5714 (from the creation of the world) is the equivalent of A.D. 1954. The Seleucid Era, widely used in the Hellenistic and Roman periods in the Near East, began in 312 B.C. when Seleucus I gained the Babylonian throne. In the same general area in Roman times, there were many provincial and city eras in restricted local use. Another widely used system was that of the Olympiads which had the equivalent of 776 B.C. as their starting point. That year would be the first year of the first Olympiad; 775 would be the second year of the first Olympiad; and, since an Olympiad was a four year period, 772 would be the first year of the second Olympiad.

In Herodotus and in the Old Testament we find reckoning by generations. This kind of thing was quite common, but the number of years assigned to a generation was not uniform. Sometimes, for example, people thought of a generation as thirty years; sometimes, forty or thirty-nine, or some other number.

Many of these different systems of reckoning were used simultaneously. In the ancient sources one finds a particular system employed by one author, and a different system by another. Various attempts were made in antiquity to synchronize the numerous chronologies. In the fourth century A.D., Eusebius, one of the first authors to employ the Christian era for dating, apparently arranged his material so that corresponding dates in the Jewish calendar, the Christian era, the Olympiads, and Roman regnal years (among others) were in parallel columns. In the first century B.C., Diodorus Siculus, who arranged his account of "world history" on an annalistic basis, spoke of "the year in which X was archon in Athens and Y and Z were consuls in Rome." In the Old Testament (*Kings* and *Chronicles*) one finds frequent synchronisms, as "In the seventh year of Jehu (of Israel) Jehoash began to reign; and he reigned forty years in Jerusalem . . . In the twenty-third year of Joash (of Judah) Jehoahaz, the son of Jehu, began to reign over Israel in Samaria, and reigned seventeen years . . . In the second year of Joash (of Israel) reigned Amaziah, the son of Joash, King of Judah. He was twenty-five years old when he began to reign, and reigned twenty-nine years in Jerusalem . . . and Amaziah (of Judah) lived fifteen years after the death of Jehoash (of Israel)."

If one attempts to construct a chronology based upon this material in *Kings* and *Chronicles*, he soon encounters seeming contradictions and gaps that pose great difficulties. It is quite possible that the kings of Israel did not use the same regnal system as the kings of Judah. Biblical scholars have been able to come to no agreement about these matters, but a very reasonable book on the subject is that of E. R. Thiele, *The Mysterious Numbers of the Hebrew Kings*, Chicago 1951.

It was certainly no easier then than now to establish a date in ancient history. Take, for example, some of the chronological data relating to the death of Philip of Macedon and the accession of Alexander the Great (336 B.C.):

Arrian, *Anabasis* (second century A.D.) says, "Philip died when Pythodemus was archon at Athens."

Diodorus Siculus calls the Athenian archon Pythodorus, and he equates the year of "Pythodorus" with the consulship of "Publius" and "Mamercus" at Rome and with the first year of the one hundred and eleventh Olympiad, which began in August 336 B.C. We know from the consular *fasti* (records) of Rome that *Mamercinus* and *Publilius* were consuls in 339!

A second-century A.D. papyrus found in Egypt in 1898 (*Oxyrhynchus Papyri*, Vol. I, no. 12) records that "in Olympiad 111 . . . the archon at Athens was Pythodelus . . . and Philip, the king of Macedon was assassinated."

A very famous inscription containing a chronological table composed in 264 B.C. has the notation, "Philip was killed, Alexander became king, in year 72, Pythodelus being archon at Athens." Year 72 is the seventy-second year before 264 B.C. (= 336). The inscription is, of course, the great Parian Marble, one fragment of which was purchased at Smyrna in the seventeenth century A.D. and eventually came into the collection of the Earl of Arundel. A second fragment, which contains the item quoted above, was found on the island of Paros itself in 1897.

Athenian inscriptions confirm that the true name of the archon was Pythodelus, and the synchronism with the 111th Olympiad assures us that the date was 336 B.C.

The archon lists, consular *fasti*, *limmu* lists, the regnal data from the Old Testament, Manetho's list of the pharaonic dynasties in Egypt, and similar compilations provide what might be called a *relative* chronology for the given country or area with which each is concerned. That is, we may know from these lists who succeeded whom, and in what order, and over a period of how many years, but frequently a relative chronology has no chronological peg (or date in terms of our chronology) on which it can be hung. Let us suppose that we had a list of one hundred consecutive archons at Athens but no information about when (in terms of our chronology) the list began or ended. This block of data would float unmoored in the abyss of time unless we could discover a synchronism with some established date. If Pythodelus were on our list, our chronological barge would be anchored at 336 B.C., and we could count backwards and forwards from that date. Sometimes an astronomical phenomenon will provide an anchor if it can be related to some historical event—the eclipse of the moon in September 330 B.C., as we shall see in the next section, dates Alexander's victory at Gaugamela.

Thus, in the immense labor of reconstructing ancient chronology the historian has had to search for synchronisms and links with astronomical phenomena in order to transform relative chronologies into *absolute* ones in which dates can be expressed in terms of our system (of years B.C. and A.D.). To cite only a few examples, the references to Assyrian kings in the Old Testament made it possible to begin with fashioning an absolute chronology for Assyria, but as detailed Assyrian and Babylonian material came to light and the inscriptions could be read, very precise dates were worked out for Mesopotamia; astronomical phenomena were brought to bear, and eventually *Biblical chronology* could be pinpointed in many instances. Today the fall of Jerusalem can be dated to August 16, 586 (Julian).

The famous Tell-el-Amarna letters of the reign of Ikhnaton provided a synchronism of Egyptian chronology with the kings of Assyria, the Kassites in Babylonia, and the Hittites in Asia Minor. Quite a number of decades ago it was possible to date with some confidence the Old Assyrian Kingdom, but the period of the Amorites and particularly of Hammurabi was in doubt. The Mari letters found in the fourth decade of this century provided a much needed link: Zimri-lim, the last king of Mari, was found to have been not only a contemporary of Ishme-Dagan of Assyria, whose period was known, but also of Hammurabi. Thus, the reign of Hammurabi, formerly dated tentatively as early as 2100 or 1900 B.C., was set pretty much in the eighteenth century B.C.

Gradually, then, the rough outlines of ancient chronology took shape, and many details, particularly of Greek and Roman history, have been worked out. But even in such comparatively recent periods troublesome little questions remain unanswered. Samples of these are given in the following sections.

Alexander the Great

In dealing with the story of Alexander the Great the historian or biographer is handicapped from the start because the best and most extensive surviving accounts of Alexander's exploits were written centuries after his death: Diodorus Siculus composed his *Universal History* in the first century B.C., while the hundred years between A.D. 50–150 is the period of Quintus Curtius Rufus (*History of Alexander the Great of Macedon*), Plutarch (*Life of Alexander*), and Arrian (*Anabasis of Alexander*); Justin's epitome of the work of Pompeius Trogus is probably a little later in date, as we have seen. Of these five, Arrian, Plutarch, and Diodorus are the most reliable, but even their accounts are sometimes difficult to harmonize or reconcile.

In general, historians have come to agree with regard to the chronology of Alexander's campaigns, although one minor question is still troublesome—the whereabouts of Alexander during the winter of 330–329 B.C. The problem may be simply stated:

Alexander defeated Darius at the battle of Arbela (Gaugamela) on October 1, 331 B.C., and he crossed the Hindu Kush range into Bactria in the early spring of 329. Between these two well-established dates he captured Babylon, Susa, and Persepolis. After resting his troops at Persepolis, he set off in pursuit of Darius. He captured Ecbatana and caught up with Darius a few hundred miles farther on. Then Alexander pushed eastward into Afghanistan. After a march of nearly 1500 miles, he arrived at the Hindu Kush.

The date of the battle of Arbela is one of the anchors of ancient chronology because it is fixed by an astronomical phenomenon, an eclipse of the moon that occurred on the night of September 20–21, 331 B.C.

PLUTARCH

LIFE OF CAMILLUS

ON THE SIXTH OF BOËDROMION, the Persians were beaten by the Greeks at Marathon; on the third, at Plataea, and also at Mycale; on the twenty-fifth, at Arbela.

LIFE OF ALEXANDER

IT HAPPENED THAT IN THE MONTH OF BOËDROMION, about the commencement of the Mysteries at Athens, there was an eclipse of the moon, the eleventh night after which, the two armies being in view of one another, Darius kept his men under arms . . . (and the battle of Arbela occurred the following day).

ARRIAN [III, 7.6]

He rested his army, and there occurred a nearly total eclipse of the moon . . . (8 + X days later the battle took place) in the archonship of Aristophanes at Athens and in the month of Pyanepsion.

The Athenian civil year began in midsummer, and in terms of our calendar the first four months of the year would be:

Hekatombaion (*July-August*)
Metageitnion (*August-September*)
Boëdromion (*September-October*)
Pyanepsion (*October-November*)

The eponymous magistrates at Athens, the archons, took office at the beginning of Hekatombaion and served for a year. We have reliable lists of the archons for this period: Aristophanes was archon 331/330, and Aristophon, 330/329. The evidence of Arrian gives us the year; and, while he and Plutarch do not agree about the month, they both mention the eclipse, which we can fix exactly.

Arrian also says (III. 22.2) that the death of Darius occurred "when Aristophon was archon at Athens and in the month Hekatombaion." This would be, then, July or early August, 330, and, if Arrian is correct, ten months intervened between the battle of Arbela and the death of Darius. What was Alexander doing in this interval? Plutarch (*Life of Alexander*) says that at Persepolis Alexander "took up his winter quarters and stayed four months to refresh his soldiers." We also have various other statements about Alexander's movements such as that of Justin (XI. 14):

"By this battle (Arbela) he gained dominion over Asia . . . after rewarding his soldiers, and allowing them to rest for thirty-four days, he took account of the spoil. . . ."

D. G. Hogarth[1] made the following calculation of Alexander's activities between October 1, 331 and July 330:

March to Babylon (300 miles), at least 40 days
Halt in Babylon, 34 days (Curtius v. 1; Justin XI. 14)
March to Susa, 20 days (Arrian III. 16)
Stay in Susa, X days

1. D. G. Hogarth, *Philip and Alexander of Macedon*, London 1897, p. 289 ff.

> March to Persepolis, 30 days
> Stay at Persepolis, 120 days (Plutarch)
> March to Ecbatana, 12+X days (Arrian III. 19)
> Stay in Ecbatana, X days
> Pursuit of Darius, 21 Days (Arrian III. 20–21)
> Total: 277+X days

Hogarth then said, "The death of Darius, therefore, took place near Shahrud, about the three hundredth day after Arbela, i.e. at the very end of July or beginning of August, 330. This . . . coincides . . . with Arrian's statement (III. 22) that the month of the murder was the Attic Hekatombaion."

After this, Alexander traveled about 1500 miles before coming to the foot of the Hindu Kush, according to Hogarth's further calculations. Moving the army at top speed, with no prolonged stops, this would have taken better than four months. But Alexander did stop several times, and no one has ever suggested that the journey took less than six months. In the eight months, however, between the beginning of August, 330 and early April, 329—when he crossed the Hindu Kush—he could have covered the required distance easily with all stops accounted for.

But there is a difficulty. The geographer Strabo (XV. 2.10) says that Alexander marched through the Paropamisadae (just south of the Hindu Kush) "about the time of the setting of the Pleiades" and arriving at the foot of the Hindu Kush, he founded a city and wintered there. (In the spring) fifteen days "after leaving the city which he had founded and his winter quarters, he came to Adrapsa, a city of Bactria."

If Alexander went into winter quarters at the foot of the Hindu Kush, it is clear that the march through the Paropamisadae took place in November (the fall setting of the Pleiades). If Plutarch and Arrian are not to be ignored, and the death of Darius occurred about the beginning of August, how can Alexander have reached the Hindu Kush by November, less than four months later?

The testimony of Arrian and Plutarch on the one hand and that of Strabo on the other is thus in conflict. Three distinguished scholars have sought to solve this problem in different ways. Hogarth decided that Alexander must have spent twenty months in Afghanistan instead of eight. He would have Alexander arriving at the foot of the Hindu Kush in November 329 (instead of November 330) and crossing the range in the spring of 328 (instead of the spring of 329). This solution has the obvious disadvantage of allowing too little time for all the events and campaigns in Bactria before Alexander's return from there in the spring of 327. W. W. Tarn (see citation below) simply chose to ignore the statement of Strabo: he preferred to think that Alexander never went into winter quarters at all, and came to the Hindu Kush in the spring of 329. C. A. Robinson, on the other hand, threw out the evidence of Plutarch and Arrian; he shortened Alexander's stay at Persepolis from four to two months, placed the death of Darius in early May instead of late July, and thus allowed Alexander enough time to reach the Hindu Kush by December. Still another attempt at solution will be found in the article reprinted here:[2]

ALEXANDER AND THE WINTER OF 330-329 B.C.

The correlation of the chronology of the expedition of Alexander the Great with the geographical position of the expedition from the beginning of 330 to the Spring of 327 has long presented great difficulties. Mr. W. W. Tarn[1] has shown very clearly that the winter of 329–328 was spent by the expedition at Zariaspa and that of 328–327 at Nautaca. Mr. Tarn does not believe that Alexander took winter quarters at all for 330–329.

Since Mr. Tarn's views are entirely in accord with Arrian's account,[2] it is doubtful if anyone now would question them for the winters of 329–328 and 328–327. There is nothing in Arrian, however, which might serve as a definite clue to the place at which Alexander passed the winter of 330–329. Wilcken[3] has suggested that Alexander's long detour to the south left little time for winter quarters, especially since Alexander is supposed to have crossed the Hindu Kush Mountains early in 329.

2. Reprinted from the *Classical Weekly*, now the *Classical World* (copyright by the Classical Association of the Atlantic States) by permission of the publishers. The original appeared in Vol. 28 (Feb. 25, 1935), pp. 124–125.

1. W. W. Tarn, *The Cambridge Ancient History*, 6, 390–395 (Cambridge: At the University Press, 1927).

2. Arrian, *Anabasis*, 4, 7. 1. 18, 2.

3. Ulrich Wilcken, *Alexander der Grosse*, 147 (Berlin and Leipzig, Quelle and Meyer, 1931). [For a review, by Professor Casper J. Kraemer, Jr., of the English translation of this work, a translation made by G. C. Richards, see *The Classical Weekly* 26. 191–192. C.K.]

Beloch[4] and Kaerst[5] place Alexander in winter quarters for 330–329 at the city of Alexandria, which he founded just south of the Hindu Kush, in the Koh Daman region. Mr. Hogarth[6] believed that Alexander wintered in Seistan. Recently Professor C. A. Robinson, Jr.[7] published his solution of this problem.

In order to allow Alexander to reach the Cabul valley by the middle of November, 330, and so to get conformity with the account of Strabo (15.2.10), Professor Robinson throws out the statement of Plutarch (Alexander 37) that Alexander allowed his army to rest for four months at Persepolis, and that of Arrian (3.22.2) which places the murder of Darius in the Attic month of Hecatombaeon. Professor Robinson maintains that Alexander left Persepolis in late March. This view automatically advances the death of Darius to about the first of May, as opposed to the accepted date (late July). This makes it possible for Professor Robinson to maintain that Alexander reached the foot of the Hindu Kush in December, and took up winter quarters there, in accordance with the statement of Strabo (15.2.10).

Careful examination of the evidence, however, will serve to render Professor Robinson's thesis untenable, for the following reasons:

1] Mr. Hogarth, accepting Plutarch's statement that Alexander remained four months at Persepolis, computed that the death of Darius occurred about the three hundredth day after the Battle of Gaugamela (or Arbela).[8] This would coincide with the date which Arrian gives— the month of Hecatombaeon. Arrian (3.22.2) mentions also that Aristophon was then archon at Athens. Now in the preceding October, when the Battle of Gaugamela (or Arbela) was fought, Aristophanes was archon. This fact Arrian tells us in 3.15.7. Hence it follows that, if Darius had been murdered at any time previous to Hecatombaeon, 330, the event must have fallen in the archonship of Aristophanes rather than in that of Aristophon.

    4. Julius Beloch, *Griechische Geschichte*[2], 3.2.319 (Berlin and Leipzig, Walter de Gruyter, 1923).
    5. J. Kaerst, *Geschichte der Hellenismus*, 1.430 (Leipzig, Teubner, 1927).
    6. D. G. Hogarth, *Philip and Alexander of Macedon*, 217 (London, Murray, 1897).
    7. Charles Alexander Robinson, Jr., "When did Alexander Reach the Hindu Kush?", *The American Journal of Philology* 51 (1931), 22–31. This is reprinted on pages 74–81 of Professor Robinson's monograph, "The Ephemerides of Alexander's Expedition" (Brown University, Providence, Rhode Island, 1932). [For a review, by Mr. Jones, of this monograph see *The Classical Weekly* 28. 118. C.K.]
    8. Hogarth, 289 (see note 6, above).

2] Then there is the matter of the reinforcements which Antipater sent from Greece[8a] after the defeat of Agis, the Spartan king, in the Autumn of 331. These soldiers appear to have caught up with Alexander either just before the siege of Artacoana (Arrian 3.25.4), or immediately after it (Quintus Curtius 6.6.35). Arrian does not specifically state that the soldiers were sent by Antipater, but the similarity of his account with that of Curtius leads me to believe that both are speaking of the same body of troops.[9] Had Alexander left Persepolis in March, the reinforcements from Antipater would never have been able to overtake him by the middle of July, as Professor Robinson maintains.

A concrete example will illustrate this. When Alexander was at Babylon in November, 331, Amyntas arrived, bringing troops from Antipater. These troops must have been despatched before any warning of the campaign of Agis, which began in the early Summer of 331.[10] It took them, then, at least five months to reach Babylon from Macedonia. The contingent which caught up with Alexander at Artacoana could not have left Macedonia[10a] before late November or December, and a conservative marching schedule would bring them to Alexander not earlier than October of 330. This would fit in very well with the scheme of Hogarth, according to which Alexander left Zadracarta in

---

8a. Antipater sent soldiers who had participated in the campaign against Agis which ended at Megalopolis. After the campaign ended, these soldiers, I believe, returned with Antipater to Macedonia. Later, after it appeared that all was quiet in the Peloponnesus, they were forwarded to Alexander. However, when they sailed from Greece to Asia Minor or came from Macedonia across the Hellespont, they could not have reached Alexander at Artacoana before October.

9. Compare Arrian 3.25.4 'Αλέξανδρος δὲ ὁμοῦ ἤδη ἔχων τὴν πᾶσαν δύναμιν ᾔει ἐπὶ Βάκτρων, ἵνα καὶ ὁ Φίλιππος ὁ Μενελάου πάρ' αὐτὸν ἀφίκετο ἐκ Μηδίας, ἔχων τούς τε μισθοφόρους ἱππέας ὧν ἡγεῖτο αὐτός, καὶ Θεσσαλῶν τοὺς ἐθελοντὰς ὑπομείναντας καὶ τοὺς ξένους τοὺς 'Ανδρομάχου; Curtius (6.6.35) Ab hac urbe [= Artacoana] digresso supplementum novorum militum occurrit. Zoilus D equites ex Graecia adduxerat; III milia ex Illyrico Antipater miserat; Thessali equites C et XXX cum Philippo erant: ex Lydia II milia et sexcenti, peregrinus miles, advenerant, CCC equites gentis eiusdem sequebantur.

Curtius's words ex Illyrico seem to mean either "Illyrian soldiery" or "soldiers from Illyricum", perhaps troops that had been guarding the frontier at Pelium. If the latter interpretation is correct, then those troops could not have left their post until they were relieved, after the war with Agis, by troops from the campaign around Megalopolis.

Arrian and Curtius are obviously speaking of the same body of troops, the soldiers that came from Antipater to Alexander. Antipater could not have sent those soldiers to Alexander until Agis was subdued.

10. Tarn, 445 (see note 1, p. 121). The troops under Amyntas undoubtedly were despatched from Macedonia, since we know that Antipater was in Macedonia at this time (the early Summer of 331) and had to move into Greece to meet Agis and his Spartans.

10a. See note 8a, above.

October.[11] Professor Robinson's view makes no allowance for these considerations.

3] "There is not a shred of evidence in Arrian or elsewhere that Alexander spent a winter in Seistan", says Professor Robinson.[12] How are we to interpret the sixty days which, Curtius (7.3.3) says, Alexander spent among the Evergetae, a period which Professor Robinson himself[13] includes in his chronological calculations? If we assume with Hogarth that Alexander left Zadracarta in October, he would have reached the land of the Evergetae in December. December and January would then have been spent in Seistan, and in February Alexander would again have taken the field, as was his custom, in winter, this time to campaign against the hill tribes, which were, in this case, those of the Candahar-Cabul district. That it was still winter Arrian (3.28.1), Curtius (7.3.11), and Diodorus (17.82.1–9) bear convincing witness.

4] Strabo's words (15.2.10), ὑπὸ Πλειάδος δύσιν, might mean either the morning or the evening setting of the Pleiades. The preposition ὑπὸ itself may mean "about the time of", just as well as "after the time of". If we assume that Strabo here means "about the time" of the evening[14] setting of the Pleiades (April), then the theory that Alexander reached the Hindu Kush in March is just as logical as Professor Robinson's view, which makes the time of arrival November.

Arrian's account of the founding of Alexandria at the foot of the Hindu Kush suggests nothing more than a very short pause, perhaps a week or two. Strabo[15] is, in fact, the only author who mentions winter quarters at this point. Since, unless the evidence of Plutarch and Arrian together is disregarded, we can not believe that Alexander arrived here in time for winter quarters, the more practical course seems to be to call into question the authority of Strabo. He was not writing a history of Alexander's expedition, and, when he examined the account of the unknown author who put Alexander's winter quarters in the Koh Daman, he did not have to consider the time element involved.

More satisfactory and more in accord with the five ancient historians

11. Hogarth, 296 (see note 6).
12. Robinson, *Ephemerides*, 76 (see note 7).
13. *Ibidem*, 79.
14. In The Loeb Classical Library version of Strabo, 7.145 (1930), Professor Horace Leonard Jones translates the phrase by "at the setting of the Pleiad. . . ." He does not indicate whether he thought of the morning setting or of the evening setting of the Pleiades. C.K.
15. See 15.2.10.

of Alexander is the following arrangement, which leaves untouched the accepted date for the death of Darius and agrees better than the scheme of Professor Robinson with the apparent chronological facts: Death of Darius, July, 330; Departure from Zadracarta, October; Arrival of reinforcements from Greece, late October or November; Rest among the Evergetae, December, 330, and January, 329; Campaigns against hill tribes, February; Arrival at the Hindu Kush, March; Crossing of the Hindu Kush, late March or April.

That it was April when Alexander arrived north of the Hindu Kush is implied in Curtius (7.4.26). He speaks of the luxuriant vegetation of part of this country. Alexander, then, was there when the growing season was most impressive (April and May). In June, when the dry season had set in, he left Bactra for the Oxus, and suffered terribly from the drought and intense heat (Curtius 7.5.1–12).

When all is said and done, it must be admitted that there is no clean and indisputable solution for this problem. In a case of this kind where proof is lacking—and there are many such—it is beneath the dignity of the historian to attempt persuasion, to argue that he is right and all others wrong. Even if his arguments secure the approval of others, he has contributed nothing to history—he has merely won a debate.

The Date of the Death of Carus

We have already made the acquaintance of the Roman emperor, Carus, and his sons, Carinus and Numerian. It was probably October of A.D. 282 when Carus became emperor. He himself died in the course of a campaign against the Persians some time in 283, but the reign was continued by his sons. Numerian died, as we have seen, in the autumn of 284, while Carinus was overcome in battle by Diocletian in the spring of 285.

That the reign of Carus and his sons began in 282 and ended in 285 is not difficult to establish. Moreover, since we now know that the *dies imperii*, the accession date, of Diocletian was November 20, 284, we can be sure that the death of Numerian occurred only a few days before that (A. H. M. Jones, *The Later Roman Empire*, Norman, Okla. 1964, Vol. I, p. 38 and Vol. II, p. 1073). The date of the death of Carus, however, is much more difficult to establish, and this is the problem which we shall consider in this section. The basic information contained in the literary sources is the following:

1] *Chronograph of 354* (A.D.). "Carus reigned 10 months (and) 5 days. He died at Seleucia in Babylonia. Carinus and Numerian reigned 2 years, 11 months, 2 days. . . ."

2] *Eutropius* (about A.D. 370). "After the death of Probus, Carus was created emperor, a native of Narbo in Gaul, who immediately made his sons, Carinus and Numerian Caesars, and reigned, in conjunction with them, two years. News being brought, while he was engaged in a war with the Sarmatians, of an insurrection among the Persians, he set out for the east, and achieved some noble exploits against that people; he routed them in the field, and took Seleucia and Ctesiphon, their noblest cities, but, while he was encamped on the Tigris, he was killed by lightning. . . ."

3] The account of Sextus Aurelius Victor, *Liber de Caesaribus* (about A.D. 360), is essentially the same except that Victor adds that an oracle forbade a Roman emperor to proceed beyond Ctesiphon, and this was the reason why Carus was struck by a thunderbolt.

4] In the *Vita Cari* of the Augustan History (of about the same vintage as Eutropius and Victor) it is stated that Carus undertook the Persian war for which Probus had been preparing; that he made his sons Caesars; that he finished most of the war against the Sarmatians before beginning that against the Persians. Carus advanced as far as Ctesiphon where he met his death, either by disease, or as the result of a fire when lightning struck his tent. "Many declare . . . [that he died] . . . because he desired to pass beyond the bounds which Fate has set up."

5] *Zonaras* (A.D. 1100). "Carus, becoming emperor, associated with himself his sons, Carinus and Numerian . . . and he campaigned against the Persians taking along one of his sons, Numerian. And he captured Ctesiphon and Seleucia . . . [The Romans were caught on low ground by the Persians who opened a dike along the Tigris and nearly flooded them out, but Carus returned to Rome with many captives and much booty . . . following this, he campaigned successfully against the Sarmatians]. He was of Gallic origin, a man skilled in warfare. Concerning his death, historians are not agreed. Some say that he fought against

the Huns and was killed, while others say that by the river Tigris . . .
his tent was struck by lightning. . . ."

In addition to the literary sources, we have the dated coins and papyri
from Egypt, inscriptions from various parts of the empire (mostly
collected in the C.I.L.—*Corpus Inscriptionum Latinarum*), and dated
rescripts of Carus, Carinus, and Numerian (mostly preserved in the
Code of Justinian).

Under the Roman Empire, the mint at Alexandria in Egypt issued
a series of coins which were dated by regnal years of the emperors.
These regnal years were geared to the Egyptian calendar as regulated by
Augustus: the year began on a date corresponding to August 29 in the
Julian calendar and ended on the following August 28. If an emperor
began to reign at any time before August 29, the period before that
date would be counted as the first year of his reign, even if it were only
a few days. Then, on August 29, the second year of the reign would
begin. For example, Probus, the predecessor of Carus, came to the
throne about July 276, and he died in the autumn of 282. The length of
his reign was therefore only a little over six years, but the Alexandrian
coins of Probus run from the year *alpha* (year 1) to the year *eta* (year 8).
Thus, the regnal years of Probus in Egypt would be:

Year 1	July–Aug. 28, 276
2	Aug. 29, 276–Aug. 28, 277
3	Aug. 29, 277–Aug. 28, 278
4	Aug. 29, 278–Aug. 28, 279
5	Aug. 29, 279–Aug. 28, 280
6	Aug. 29, 280–Aug. 28, 281
7	Aug. 29, 281–Aug. 28, 282
8	Aug. 29, 282–Oct. 282

Also the papyrus contracts and official documents in Egypt would
be dated in the same way.

Dated Greek and Latin inscriptions, from various parts of the empire,
usually include *a*] the number of times the emperor has held the
consulship, and *b*] his grants of the tribunician power, conferred
annually. A variety of lists, consular *fasti* and the like, have given us
positive information about the date and order of the consuls. The
consulship began on the first of January. Probus, for example, was
consul for the first time in January 277, and the dates of his succeeding

consulships were II, Jan. 278; III, Jan. 279; IV, Jan. 281; V, Jan. 282. Thus, an inscription dated in his second consulship must fall in the year 278; his third, between Jan. 279 and the end of December, 280, and so on.

The tribunician power, which was conferred annually, was in some periods dated from December 10; but in others, from the anniversary of the emperor's accession. Thus, if the December 10th system were being used, an emperor like Probus who came to the throne in July would have his first grant of the tribunician power from July to the following December, and his second grant would run from December 10 of that year to December 10 of the following year. If the anniversary system were in use, the first year of the tribunician power would run from July, in this case, to the following July. Under the first system Probus would be tr. p. I from July–Dec. 10, 276; tr. p. II, Dec. 10, 276–Jan. 1, 277; and tr. p. II cos. I from Jan. 1, 277–Dec. 10, 277, etc. Under the second system, he would be tr. p. I from July 276–Jan. 1, 277; tr. p. I cos. I from Jan. 1, 277–July 277; and tr. p. II cos. I from July 277 to Jan. 1, 278, etc.

The imperial rescripts, replies of the emperors to judicial inquiries addressed to them, are to be found in the Code of Justinian and related documents. These are dated by day, month, and consulship, and sometimes the place where the emperor happened to be when the response was given may be included. For example, the earliest dated rescript of Diocletian that we possess is from Oct. 15, 284. If the date is correct, Numerian must have been dead by that time. Unfortunately, the manuscript tradition for the rescripts is not entirely trustworthy, and in many instances, it is quite corrupt. Thus, the dates from the rescripts must be used with caution.

With all this in mind, let us examine the following article, published in the *American Journal of Philology* (July 1938), which attempted to establish a date for the death of Carus:[3]

A CHRONOLOGICAL PROBLEM: THE DATE OF THE DEATH OF CARUS

In view of the fact that the available historical evidence for the years 282–283 A.D. is not extensive, the determination of the chronology for

---

3. Reprinted from the *American Journal of Philology* by permission of the publishers. The original appeared in Vol. 59 (1938), pp. 338–342.

the reign of the Roman Emperor Marcus Aurelius Carus presents many problems. One of the most difficult of these problems is concerned with the date of Carus' death, an event which took place some time in the latter part of the year 283. Vogt[1] and Domaszewski,[2] basing their chronological calculations upon the evidence of the Alexandrian coinage and the material contained in the so-called "Chronograph of 354," reached the conclusion that Carus met his death before August 29 of that year. Their arguments may be summarized as follows:

1] To all appearances, the Alexandrian coinage of Carus does not go beyond the year A, the first year. At any rate, no coins of the year B are known. Vogt therefore assumes that Carus reigned sometime between August 28, 282 and August 29, 283.[3] The first year (A) of Carinus and Numerian, the sons of Carus who were associated in the imperial government with their father, corresponds to the first year of Carus, although at the beginning of his reign Carus gave them only the rank of Caesars. During the course of the year A Carinus was made an Augustus, while Numerian was not accorded this title until some time in the year B, the second year.[4] Coins of Carinus and also of Numerian for the year 3 are known, indicating that the brothers continued to rule after August 28, 284.

2] Substantiating evidence for the theory that Carus ruled only one year may be found in the "Chronograph of 354" which records the length of his reign as ten months and five days. Therefore, as far as Carus is concerned, the coin dates and the "Chronograph" are in agreement.

3] Basing his conclusions on the foregoing evidence Domaszewski calculated the approximate dates for the reign of Carus as September 7, 282 to July 11, 283.[5] Historians generally agree in placing the death of Numerian in the autumn of 284 and that of Carinus in the spring of 285.

Nevertheless, in spite of the apparently indisputable testimony of the Alexandrian coinage and the "Chronograph of 354" regarding the brevity of Carus' reign, there is much to be said for the theory of the older historians headed by Schiller,[6] who thought that Carus did not die

1. J. Vogt, Die alexandrinischen Münzen, Stuttgart, 1924, p. 166.
2. A. von Domaszewski, "Die Daten der Scriptores Historiae Augustae," Sitz. Heid. Akad., VIII (1917), pp. 34–35.
3. Vogt, op. cit., p. 166. The Alexandrian regnal year ended August 28 and began August 29.
4. Ibid., p. 166.
5. Domaszewski, op. cit., p. 34.
6. H. Schiller, Geschichte der römischen Kaiserzeit, Gotha, 1883, I, p. 884.

until December, 283.[7] Moreover, a study of the epigraphic sources, hitherto disregarded, lends strong support to this earlier opinion. The following table of the dates at which Carus presumably received consular and tribunician honors will serve to demonstrate this point:

Sept. 282[8]–Jan. 283   tr. p. I cos. I — *C. I. L.* II, 1117, 4760;
                         VIII, 968;
                         E. E. VIII, 740;
                         A. E. (1923) 16, 103.[9]

Jan. 283–Sept. 283   tr. p. I cos. II — *C. I. L.* II, 3660, 4102;
                      E. E. VIII, 227.

Sept. 283–Dec.(?) 283   tr. p. II cos. II — *C. I. L.* VIII, 5332, 10250,
                         12522.

Mattingly has already put forth arguments to show that in the third century the tribunician power was renewed on the anniversary of the date on which each emperor first received it rather than on December 10 as Mommsen supposed.[10] The inscriptions noted in the table above can be interpreted only as additional proof for Mattingly's theory. Lest it be urged that this is the merest coincidence, it is only necessary to point to the coins and inscriptions of the preceding emperor Probus which tell the same story, demonstrating beyond any question that Probus, who first received the tribunician power in July 276,[11] annually renewed this power in the month of July and not in December.[12]

7. They based their theory upon a rescript of Carus (*Cod. Greg.*, II, 2, 2) dated in that month and year.

8. It is possible that Carus did not actually become emperor until October (Domaszewski, *op. cit.*, p. 34).

9. *A. E.*: "Année Épigraphique" in *Revue Archéologique*.

10. H. Mattingly, "Notes on the Chronology of the Roman Emperors from Valerian to Diocletian," *Jour. Eg. Arch.*, XIII (1927), p. 14; "Tribunicia Potestate," *Jour. Rom. Studies*, XX (1930), pp. 78–91; Mommsen, *Röm. Staat.*, II, p. 796.

11. H. F. Stobbe, "Tribunat der Kaiser," *Philologus*, XXXII (1873), p. 78.

12. Probus was consul in 277, 278, 279, 281, 282 (Pauly-Wissowa, II, p. 2519), and we may correlate his consulships and grants of the tribunician power as follows:

July 276–Jan. 277	tr. p. I		— *C. I. L.* II, 4881
Jan. 277–July		I cos. I	— II, 1116; XI, 1178
July–Jan. 278	II	I	— III, 8707
Jan. 278–July	II	II	
July–Jan. 279	III	II	— XII, 5437, 5511;
			E. E. VII, 693.
Jan. 279–July	III	III	
July–Jan. 280	IV	III	
Jan. 280–July	IV	III	

If Carus' second grant of the tribunician power *had* been conferred in December 282, it would have been impossible for an inscription to record TR. P. I COS. II (as we find it in *C. I. L.* II, 3660, 4102; *E. E.* VIII, 227) since he would have to have been TR. P. II before becoming COS. II. Moreover, if this had been the case, we should expect to find him as TR. P. II COS. I for the period December 10, 282–January 1, 283. No inscriptions of the TR. P. II COS. I type are known, however, and since all the evidence points in the opposite direction, it may be concluded that Carus was not made TR. P. II until September 283, the anniversary of his accession. At that date, therefore, Carus must have been still alive.

Although there is apparently no way to put aside the evidence of the Alexandrian coinage except to produce strong arguments for disregarding it,[13] the "Chronograph of 354" presents no such obstacle. It is a well-known fact that the "Chronograph" is seldom accurate. The length of the reign of Carinus and Numerian as given in the "Chronograph" is 2 years, 11 months and 2 days. This estimate is too long by at least five months. According to the same chronicle Diocletian and Maximian ruled 21 years, 11 months and 12 days. Actually they reigned less than 21 years. It is not advisable, therefore, to use the "Chronograph" for important chronological details.

The theory that Carus died in July 283 cannot be reconciled with the evidence of the literary sources. The ancient historians of the fourth century A.D. agree that Carus was killed by a bolt of lightning during a severe thunderstorm after his victorious army had penetrated Persian

July–Jan. 281	V	III— *C. I. L.* II, 3738
Jan. 281–July	V	IV
July–Jan. 282	VI	IV— II, 1673
Jan. 282–July	VI	V — Cohen, 460 (Vol. VI, Probus)
July–Oct. (?)	VII	V

If a similar table is worked out on the supposition that the tribunician power was renewed on Dec. 10, it will be found that the inscriptions *C.I.L.* II, 1116 and XI, 1178 cannot be used since there will be no place for tr. p. I cos. I. More important, however, is the fact that the coin Cohen 460 (tr. p. VI cos V) will not fit into such a system. Therefore the solution offered in the above table is the most satisfactory.

13. Mattingly, *Jour. Eg. Arch.*, XIII (1927), p. 16 implies that coins of the year B of Carus *have* been found, but this must be a misstatement. One particular point in connection with the Alexandrian coinage should be noted, however. Numerian does not become an Augustus until some time in his *second year*. If Carus had died in July, as Domaszewski supposed, it is difficult to see why Numerian did not appear as Augustus on the coins late in the first year or from the very outset of the second year. As long as Numerian remains a Caesar, we should expect to find coins of his father Carus as Augustus since Numerian probably was proclaimed his successor by the Persian expeditionary force.

territory as far as Ctesiphon.[14] This story in itself gives us the date for the event. Thunderstorms occur in Mesopotamia frequently during the winter months (November–March) and *never* in July.[15] Furthermore, Diocletian, who was with Carus at this time, was, in later life, notoriously afraid of thunderstorms, and it is quite likely that having witnessed Carus' accident he feared that a similar fate might overtake him.[16]

Another bit of epigraphical evidence which strengthens the supposition that Carus was still alive in the autumn of 283 is to be found in *C. I. L.* VIII, 10283 in which Numerian as Caesar is mentioned as *consul designatus*. We know that Numerian was consul for the first time in 284.[17] The *consules designati* were usually announced in the latter part of the year;[18] and therefore the inscription can be dated in the autumn of 283. If Numerian was still Caesar at that time, his father cannot have been dead.

The conclusion that Carus reigned until nearly the end of 283 is amply justified by the arguments advanced above. The last rescript of his reign is dated in December of that year,[19] and it seems probable that his death occurred in that month.

From what has been said thus far, it should be clear that as of 1938 one might, depending upon the weight he assigned to the various bits of evidence, conclude that Carus died either in the summer of 283 or in December of that year. If the statement regarding the length of Carus' reign given by the Chronograph of 354 was felt to be unreliable, then only the Egyptian evidence needed careful consideration.

True, neither coins nor papyri of the second year of Carus were known. In the year *alpha* (the first year) the Alexandrian mint issued coins of Carus as Augustus; coins of Carinus, first as Caesar and later as Augustus; coins of Numerian as Caesar only. There were undated and obviously posthumous coins of Carus which might have been issued late in the first year or sometime in the second. These bore the

14. Eutropius, IX, 18; Victor, *De Caesaribus*, 38, 3; Festus, XXIV; and others. Lightning struck Carus' tent, and he perished in the flames.

15. Professor A. E. R. Boak of the University of Michigan has been so kind as to forward to me the opinions of Professor LeRoy Waterman and Professor Clark Hopkins, both well acquainted with the climate of Mesopotamia, who are agreed that a July thunderstorm would be out of the question entirely.

16. Constantine the Great, *Oratio ad Sanctorum Coetum*, Chap. 25.

17. Pauly–Wissowa, II, p. 2513.

18. Mommsen, *op. cit.*, I, p. 558.

19. *Cod. Greg.*, II, 2, 2.

portrait of Carus on the obverse (heads side) with the legend (inscription): "To the Divine Carus Augustus." Two different reverse (tails) types were known: one was an altar, and the other was an eagle with wings spread; and both types were accompanied by the legend Ἀφιέρωσις (Hallowed). For the year *beta* (second) and the year *gamma* (third), there were coins of Carinus as Augustus. As for Numerian, the coins of the second year showed him first as Caesar and later as Augustus; for the third year he was shown consistently as Augustus. Three dated papyri from the spring of 283 (year 1) showed Carus and Carinus as Augusti, and Numerian as Caesar; the only other known papyrus was dated in August 284 (year 2) and bore the names of Carinus and Numerian as Augusti. Thus, it could be argued, from lack of evidence, that Carus could have been alive after August 29, 283; that possibly the first series of coins issued in the second year might not have been struck until early in 284, weeks or months after his death.

The evidence of the imperial rescripts found in the Code of Justinian was ambiguous, to say the least. Between March 283 and January 284 there were eight rescripts, six of them dated between September 9–December 22, 283, which were designated as having been issued in the name of the three rulers, Carus, Carinus, and Numerian. In 284 there were rescripts dated January 16, February 14, April 12, and September 12 issued in the name of Carinus and Numerian only. This would have been consistent with the theory that Carus survived until December 283, if it had not been for the fact that the pattern was spoiled by two rescripts of 284 (January 24 and March 15) which were issued in the name of all three rulers! The rescripts, then, had to be ruled out as evidence for either the July or December date for the death of Carus.

The matter was finally resolved in 1960 with the publication of a papyrus dated October 25, 283 (A. E. R. Boak and H. C. Youtie, *The Archive of Aurelius Isidorus*, Ann Arbor 1960, pp. 181–182, no. 33). The date reads "Year 2 of Carinus and Numerian." Carus was already dead!

VI

A Word about Documents

FOR our purposes in this chapter we shall define documents as ancient writings inscribed on stone, metal, clay, papyrus, pottery, leather, parchment, or any of the other materials used in antiquity to receive writing. Unlike the formal histories of Herodotus or Thucydides, for example, these documents in the majority of cases were not produced for posterity or intended as historical records. They were devised for the (then) present rather than the future, and for this reason they are all the more valuable as historical evidence. In other words, many types of documents are primary sources in the best sense, free of the bias, deliberate falsification, errors of fact and interpretation, and selectivity of material that often mar the formal histories. This is not always true, of course, but for the most part the modern historian of antiquity can use the documents and make his own mistakes rather than compounding those of his ancient counterparts.

The documents fall roughly into two classes: public and private. In the first category, without attempting to be comprehensive, one might list law codes, and individual laws, decrees, and resolutions emanating from rulers and legislative bodies; treaties and diplomatic correspondence; administrative records, including official letters and petitions; display inscriptions (as, for example, those of the Assyrian and Egyptian kings); dedicatory inscriptions for buildings, statuary, votive objects, and the like; various honorary and commemorative texts; and miscellaneous inscriptions—boundary markers, Roman mile stones, and many others too numerous to mention.

In the private category are business records and accounts; memoranda; legal documents belonging to individuals—wills, contracts, agreements, deeds of divorce, and so forth; private letters; and sepulchral inscriptions.

Sometimes a single document will be important and highly informative; in other cases, a group of documents must be studied in the mass in order to realize their full value. In the first instance, the Ashurbanipal inscription relating to Gyges is a good example of a single text of some importance, although it should also be mentioned that display inscriptions of this type share many of the faults of the formal histories. As for groups of texts, the Sumerian administrative documents discussed below illustrate the potential importance of the type of evidence in which individual documents may be insignificant and singularly uninformative but highly revealing when treated with others of the same class.

Even the beginning student of ancient history soon becomes familiar with certain famous documents and can readily appreciate their utility in historical reconstruction. The Bisitun inscription and the Rosetta Stone were fundamental to the decipherment of ancient scripts, but the Bisitun text also provided an indispensable narrative of the events connected with the accession of Darius the Great. The Code of Hammurabi, our most complete Mesopotamian law code, is known only from the stones on which it was inscribed. We have already discussed the Parian Marble, a valuable chronological compilation, while in the realm of official correspondence one immediately recalls the Tell-el-Amarna letters or the great archives of Assyrian royal correspondence. The Mari letters helped to solve a chronological problem, the date of Hammurabi, but they have also told us much about diplomacy, military strategy, and imperial administration in that age. One of the best-known inscriptions of the later Roman period is Diocletian's great Edict of Prices issued in A.D. 301; this has been pieced together from many fragments in Greek and Latin mostly discovered in various parts of the Roman East. Equally familiar is the *Res Gestae*, sometimes called the last will and testament of

Augustus, which was composed in A.D. 14. In autobiographical form Augustus reviewed his public career from the death of Julius Caesar in 44 B.C. to very nearly his own demise fifty-eight years later. For the historical details of the period and for a description of the evolution of the Principate under Augustus, this inscription is invaluable. The original text was inscribed on bronze tablets which were placed in the mausoleum of Augustus in Rome, but copies in both Greek and Latin were distributed throughout the empire and inscribed on stone for public display in many major cities. Our fullest version comes from the wall of the Temple of Rome and Augustus in Ankara, Turkey, and the text is commonly known as the Monumentum Ancyranum.

Documents, of course, present their own unique problems. Texts are seldom complete. Damaged, worn, broken, fragmentary, they often fail us at the most crucial points. Scholars often attempt restorations of the texts; naturally, they are most successful with simple, formulaic material, but the unfavorable odds increase as the text is longer, more unusual, and—regrettably—more important. To deal with documents special knowledge, training, and experience are required. One must know the scripts and the languages; he must be expert in the grammar, vocabulary, and formulae peculiar to the particular class of documents with which he proposes to work. A high degree of specialization is inevitably required for this kind of research.

In order to illustrate in part what has been said above, we may now turn to a few examples of types of documents and the manner in which the historian may exploit them.

Administrative Documents

Our most abundant and detailed ancient governmental records with regard to administration and economic organization come from the cuneiform texts of Mesopotamia and the papyri and ostraka of Egypt. A single text may tell us very little, but thousands carefully organized and analyzed will yield information not available from any other source. The example given here is merely intended to suggest the possibilities, nor should the reader forget that it could have just as easily have been drawn from the papyri.[1]

Some individuals seem to have a passion for organization. What is more, history occasionally reveals whole societies in which orderliness approaches a national characteristic. Such a group were the Sumerians, the founders of civilization in the lower Tigris-Euphrates Valley.

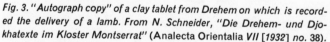

Fig. 3. "Autograph copy" of a clay tablet from Drehem on which is record-ed the delivery of a lamb. From N. Schneider, "Die Drehem- und Djo-khatexte im Kloster Montserrat" (Analecta Orientalia *VII [1932] no. 38).*

To say that the Sumerians were methodical is to understate the case. They invented a system of writing, the cuneiform, which was to be used by many different groups over a wide area long after the Sumerians had disappeared. Religious, literary and scientific works were to be written in the cuneiform, but that was not the purpose for which the

1. Reprinted from *Archaeology* by permission of the publishers. The original appeared in Vol. 9 (1956), pp. 16–21.

Sumerians originally devised it. They invented writing in order to keep track of things: their cattle and sheep and grain. This is clearly demonstrated by the fact that the earliest known Sumerian documents are lists of possessions.

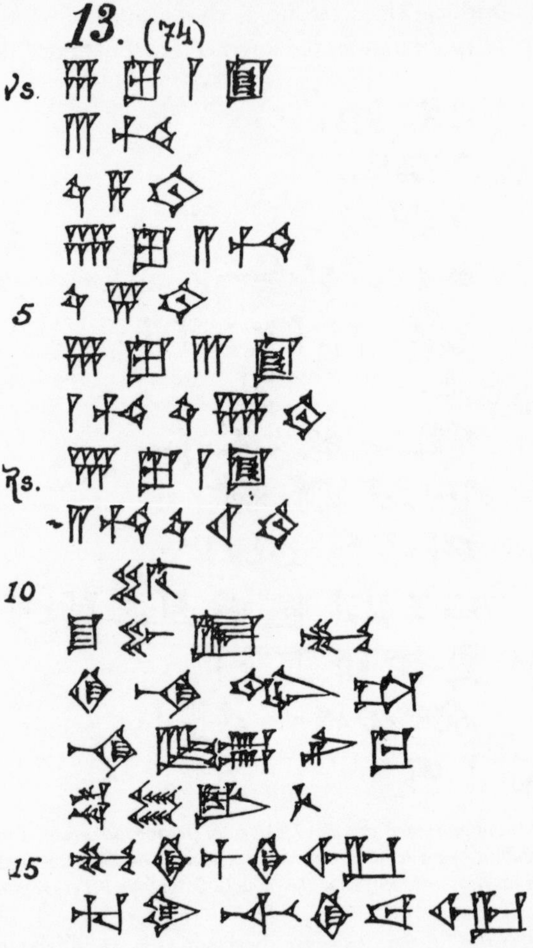

Fig. 4. A copy of a Drehem tablet on which a number of deliveries, covering several days, is recorded. From N. Schneider, op. cit. (no. 13).

The record-keeping of the Sumerians began in the fourth millennium B.C. and continued throughout their whole history. Most of the Sumerian texts we now possess are "economic," the business records of temple and palace. The bulk of these texts dates from the very end of the

Sumerian period, the era of the Third Dynasty of Ur, just before 2000 B.C. Not only do the records attain their greatest volume in this last blaze of Sumerian glory, but also they become most detailed. It was not enough, for example, to note the receipt of an ox, but it must be stated whether it was a grain-fed ox, a grass-fed ox, a young ox, an old ox, or whether it belonged in any one of a dozen other categories.

This is not to suggest that the Sumerians were just congenital enumerators. Rather, their orderliness was the product of necessity. In the first place, ancient Mesopotamia could support a dense population only if the canal system was kept in repair to foster irrigation and prevent floods. This involved the organization and direction of labor; the whole country must be run like an efficient machine. Secondly, the Sumerians lived in a theocracy in which most of the land and its animals and products belonged to the gods. Throughout most of the Sumerian period earthly rulers were considered but the bailiffs of the gods: they as well as their subjects had to render careful accounts of stewardship to supernatural masters. With a touch of cynicism we may wonder whether it was mere coincidence that the most meticulous record-keeping occurred when the kings of the Third Dynasty of Ur had assumed divine status for themselves.

The theocracy forced the Sumerians to *count*, but conditions of life in the valley also forced them to *figure*. Though at present we have no Sumerian mathematical texts, the great development of mathematics in the succeeding Age of Hammurabi suggests that the foundations had already been laid by the Sumerians. It is instructive that the Sumerians became imbued with the concepts of number and organization to such an extent that their thinkers, the priests, postulated an orderly cosmos in which numbers were assigned even to the gods.

The careful record-keeping of the Sumerians is best illustrated by the tens of thousands of clay tablets from the Ur III period which constitute the accounts of temple and palace officials. The great ledgers from Ur itself with their endless lists of workers, materials and supplies conjure up a picture of the capital as a busy anthill of productive activity. From other towns—Lagash, Umma, Nippur, Adab—come myriads of texts bearing on temple industry, agricultural work, transportation and trade. Most revealing of all, however, are the texts from Drehem, the site of the so-called cattle market of Nippur.

Drehem is the modern name for a mound a few miles southeast of

Nippur which has recently been rediscovered by Thorkild Jacobsen of The Oriental Institute, University of Chicago. Records from its archives, however, were first identified nearly fifty years ago (about 1908) after natives in search of antiquities had broken into the mound and plundered the archives, selling the tablets to dealers in Baghdad. As a result, the Drehem texts, numbering perhaps a hundred thousand, were parceled out in small lots to buyers all over the world. Possessed today by museums, libraries and private collectors, they are scattered from Paris to Tokyo, from London to Kansas City. Thousands of the Drehem texts have been published, mostly in the form of "autograph copies" (Figure 3), but thousands more await study and publication. Furthermore, the location of many of the tablets is at present unknown to scholars.

Although a complete picture of the operations at Drehem in Sumerian times cannot be reconstructed until more texts have been made available, it is nevertheless possible to comprehend the general outline of activities there. The procedures followed are reasonably clear, and some of the accounts can be reconstituted at least in part.

Drehem is thought to have functioned as a receiving depot for animals intended mostly for official use in the city of Nippur. Cattle, sheep, goats, and other beasts were brought or sent to Drehem by officials, by private persons, or by royal order. These animals were in turn paid out for various religious and secular purposes. For each transaction, whether receipt or disbursement, a separate record was made; such records were then incorporated with others into daily, monthly, and even yearly summaries.

The whole process may be clarified if we follow it, step by step, with illustrations drawn from actual texts. Figure 3 is an "autograph copy" of a Drehem text which may be translated as follows:

> Verso   1 lamb,
> on the 15th day,
> delivered (by) royal (order)
> In-ta-è-a (personal name)
> Recto   took in charge.
> Gìr, ᵈNanna-
> ma-ba, scribe.
> Month of Eating Gazelles (First Month);
> Year after the Divine Shu-Sîn,

the King, Si-ma-

núm (the city) destroyed.

Edge   (total) 1 sheep.

This text, then, is a record of one lamb to be credited to the royal account, brought to Drehem and taken in charge there by an official named In-ta-è-a on the fifteenth day of the first month of the fourth year of King Shu-Sîn (*ca.* 2050 B.C.). The function of the scribe, ^dNanna-ma-ba, who is designated as *gìr*, is somewhat uncertain, but he is likely either to have brought the animal to Drehem or to have caused it to be sent there.

Figure 4 shows a summary of a number of transactions similar to the one we have just considered. In this latter record, dated in the twelfth month of the forty-fourth year of King Shulgi (about fifteen years earlier than the text of Figure 3), deliveries on several days are recorded:

Verso   6 sheep, 1 ewe,

3 kids

on the 4th day;

8 sheep, 2 kids,

on the 5th day;

6 sheep, 3 ewes,

1 kid on the 8th day;

Recto   7 sheep, 1 ewe,

2 kids on the 11th day.

(Total) 39 (this is, of course, an error)

šu-gìd (for) the kitchen

from Na-lu$_5$ (personal name)

Na-ša$_6$ took in charge.

Month

Year

Na-ša$_6$, the receiving official, occupies the same post as that later held by In-ta-è-a in the first transaction considered (Figure 3), but this second text is a summary compiled from records of the deliveries of Na-lu$_6$ on the fourth, fifth, eighth, and eleventh days. Each of these deliveries would have been recorded on a tablet like that shown in Figure 1. The Sumerian term *šu-gìd* is sometimes rendered "tax" or "duty," although it may refer to animals destined to be killed for their hides while their carcasses were sent to the kitchen to feed temple and other employees. In the case of the seven sheep, one ewe and two kids brought in on the eleventh day, we know from another tablet that they and an ox were duly forwarded to the kitchen.

After animals were brought to Drehem, the receiving official might dispose of them in one of several ways. Some animals might be sent to Nippur for sacrifice; others might go to the kitchen, the *é-dub-ba* (warehouse?), or the *é-uzu-ga* (bird-house?) where hawks and other predators

Fig. 5. Tablet recording the transfer of six lambs and one kid. (Science Museum, St. Paul, Minn.)

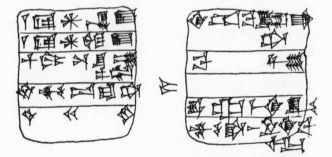

Fig. 6. A copy of a tablet recording an expenditure of two lambs for sacrifice. From H. de Genouillac, Tablettes de Dréhem (Museé du Louvre, Département des Antiquités Orientales) Vol. II, plate 44, no. 5594.

were kept. Still others, not needed at the moment, might be sent out to the sheepfold or the corrals, or transferred to the custody of another official for disposal. A tablet recording a transfer of this latter kind is shown in Figure 5.

Thus far we have seen examples of texts recording the delivery or transfer of animals, but for each record of this kind there was also a record of expenditure. Figure 6 is the text of an expenditure by a receiving official named Ab-ba-ša₆-ga. It is dated on the twentieth day of the eleventh month of the sixth year of King Amar-Sîn (who reigned between Shulgi and Shu-Sîn). The text reads:

Verso	1 lamb (for) En-lil (a god)
	1 lamb (for) Nin-lil (a goddess)
	Maš-tur, the cup-bearer, *maškim*
	(taken) from the (daily) deliveries
	on the 20th day
Recto	from Ab-ba-ša₆-ga
	was expended.
	Month
	Year
Edge	(total) 2 (lambs)

Maš-tur as *maškim* would be the recipient of the lambs at Nippur.

Expenditures were also summarized at the end of the month. Figure 7 is an "autograph copy" of a large tablet in the British Museum listing in six columns the daily expenditures of Ab-ba-ša₆-ga during the eleventh month of the sixth year of Amar-Sîn. Columns I–IV give the expenditures day by day; columns V–VI show summaries ending with a grand total of 109 animals and the date. The expenditures of the twentieth day may be seen at the bottom of column III, lines 22–27. A comparison of this section with the text of Figure 6 will reveal the identity of the two transactions.

Figure 8 is a photograph of the obverse of a very large account which summarizes day by day, and month by month, the receipt of dead animals at the *é-dub-ba* (warehouse?) for an entire year (Shu-Sîn 6).

In addition to the types of accounting already mentioned, there were also "balanced accounts" in which an official would summarize both his receipts and disbursements for the period of a month, a year, or several years.

From the fact that duplicates of Drehem texts are known to exist and that "Drehem" texts have been found at Adab, Umma and Ur, we may infer that duplicates of receipts were usually made. One copy would be retained at Drehem and the other would go into the records of the place from which the animals had been sent. It is also known that blank tablets were made in molds in advance of the day's business and that there were standard sizes of tablets for the different types of records.

COLUMN I.   COLUMN II.   COLUMN III.

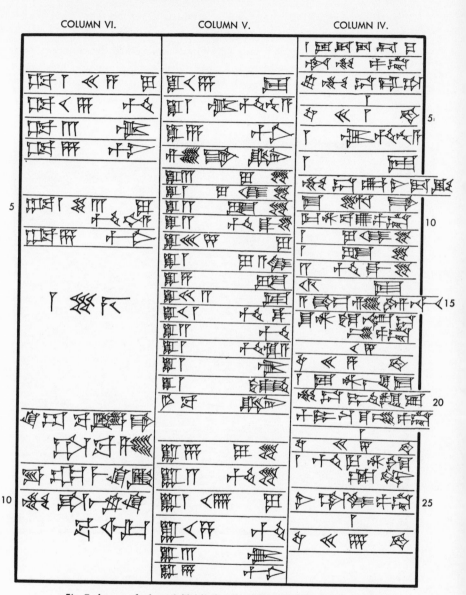

Fig. 7. A copy of a large tablet listing the daily expenditures of an official over the period of one month. At left, obverse; at right, reverse of tablet. From Cuneiform Texts from Babylonian Tablets in the British Museum, *Part 32 (1912) plates 10-11, no. 103412.*

When a record was inscribed on a tablet, the tablet was "filed" in a basket. These baskets were ultimately removed to the archives, where each basket was provided with a clay label attached to the container by a string. The label would be inscribed with a colophon which would summarize the contents of the basket: "Receipts of X for the year Y," etc. Such an archive label is shown in Figure 9.

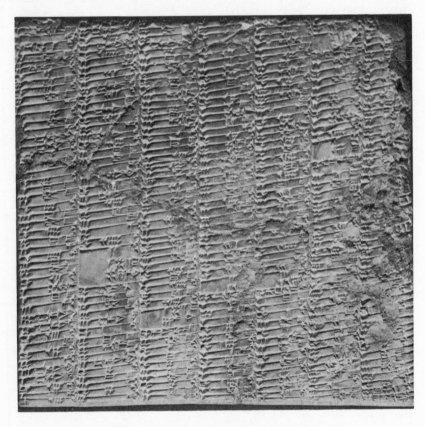

Fig. 8.

The careful bookkeeping of the Drehem scribes is typical of the meticulousness with which Sumerian business records were kept. The tablets which deal with agricultural activity or with palace industry are equally detailed. These are rich sources for the economic historian, matched only by the papyri of Graeco-Roman Egypt. To the humble

Na-ša6, Ab-ba-ša6-ga, and In-ta-è-a of the twenty-first century B.C., the equally humble scholar of the twentieth century A.D. is duly grateful.

Private Documents

As with the administrative texts, so also with the private documents the greatest rewards come from the study of a group of texts, and of these the most interesting class is that of the individual or family archive. Among the well-known archives in the papyri are those of Sarapion (J. Schwartz, *Les archives de Sarapion et de ses fils*, Cairo 1961), dating from

Fig. 9.

the period A.D. 90–133; Aurelius Isidorus (A. E. R. Boak and H. C. Youtie, *The Archive of Aurelius Isidorus*, Ann Arbor 1960), ranging from A.D. 267–324; and Abinnaeus (H. I. Bell *et al.*, *The Abinnaeus Archive*, Oxford 1962), second quarter of the fourth century A.D. The Sarapion archive includes petitions, declarations to officials, receipts, contracts, accounts, and letters. It gives a picture of the life of an Egyptian farmer during a fairly prosperous period. Aurelius Isidorus, another Egyptian farmer but in the less fortunate days of Diocletian and Constantine, left behind nearly 150 papyri which show us a villager beset with taxes and liturgies (forced public services). Abinnaeus was a Roman officer in Egypt in the generation after Aurelius Isidorus. The more than eighty documents in his archive are partly official, partly personal. Abinnaeus' circumstances were a little more favorable than those of Aurelius, but he, too, had his troubles with the bureaucracy.

Of all papyrus archives, however, the best-known and properly so is that of Zenon, first studied in detail by M. I. Rostovtzeff (*A Large Estate in Egypt in the Third Century B.C.*, Madison 1922). In the reign of Ptolemy II, Zenon, a Greek from Caria, served as the principal agent managing the very extensive private affairs of Apollonius, the *dioecetes* (secretary of the treasury). Most of the documents, and there are more than a thousand, have to do with Zenon's management of a huge estate belonging to Apollonius and with the founding of a town called Philadelphia which was to be populated by Greco-Macedonian colonists. Although Apollonius fell from favor and may have been liquidated by his royal master, the farm, the town, and Zenon continued to prosper. The story told by the documents is an interesting one, and not without its moments of humor.

The Old Babylonian archive discussed below has much in common with those of Sarapion or Aurelius Isidorus. It antedates them by many centuries; its documents were written on clay rather than papyrus; and its language is Akkadian rather than Greek, but the various types of records it contains are much the same as those of its Greek cousins.[2]

BY THE RIVERS OF BABYLON SAT WE DOWN

Thirty-eight centuries ago in the thriving Babylonian town of Dilbat there lived an obscure little farmer named Idin-Lagamal. Today, Dilbat is almost forgotten,[1] but nearly four-score broken and crumbling clay tablets remain to tell the story of Idin-Lagamal and his descendants.[2]

2. Reprinted from *Agricultural History* by permission of the publishers. The original appeared in Vol. 25 (1951), pp. 1–9.

---

1. The site of Dilbat bears the modern name of Dêläm, and the place is so unimportant that it does not even appear on ordnance maps. Dilbat was about 17 miles south of Babylon. Hammurabi spoke of the "plantations of Dilbat and the granaries of Urash" there. Rassam dug briefly at Dêläm in the late nineteenth century and brought out the first of the tablets on which this article is based; the others were found by natives and sold to dealers. Hormuzd Rassam, *Asshur and the Land of Nimrod* (New York, 1879), 265.

2. Autographed texts of the Dilbat contracts may be found in M. J. E. Gautier, *Archives d'une famille de Dilbat* (Cairo, 1908; these texts are henceforth cited as G 1, G 2, etc.); in

Meager though the evidence may seem and limited in scope, these surviving fragments of the family archives, most of them dated contracts, may be employed to produce something more than an outline of four generations of economic activity.

Idin-Lagamal was born about 1900 B.C.[3] His father's name was Ili-amrâni, and his two brothers were called Bêl-ilum and Aḫukinum.[4] Ili-amrâni may have been a native of Dilbat, but it is quite possible that he had drifted into Babylonia about the middle of the twentieth century with the Semitic tribesmen who were to establish their capital at Babylon and found the Amorite or Old Babylonian dynasty there around 1890. At any rate, Ili-amrâni had lived in Dilbat long enough to acquire property in town and some agricultural land as well, and this, according to custom, had been divided among his sons at his death.[5]

Dilbat was the center of a rich farming community. The town itself stood on the banks of the Araḫtum, one of the major Babylonian canals,

---

3. The chronological system here employed is that favored by Professor George G. Cameron, University of Michigan. There is now little doubt that Hammurabi reigned in the eighteenth century B.C. The birth of Idin-Lagamal is dated about 1900 B.C. because he was obviously an adult by the fourth year of Sumu-abum (c. 1876 B.C.). See footnote 9 below.

4. Bêl-ilum is a witness in PSBA; Aḫukinum in G 4.

5. The appearance of Bêl-ilum and Aḫukinum as witnesses in PSBA and G 4 respectively suggests that the family homestead was involved.

Arthur Ungnad, vol. 7 of *Vorderasiatische Shriftdenkmäler* (Leipzig, 1909; cited henceforth as U 1, U 2, etc.); one tablet is recorded in the *Proceedings of the Society for Biblical Archaeology*, 29: 275–276 (1907; cited henceforth as PSBA); and there are two contracts in the British Museum series called *Cuneiform Texts from Babylonian Tablets*, one in vol. 4 (cited here as CT IV 46e) and one in vol. 6 (cited here as CT VI 48b). A few Dilbat texts are to be found in François Thureau-Dangin, *Lettres et contrats de l'époque de la première dynastie babylonienne* (Musée du Louvre, *Textes cunéiformes*, t. 1, Paris, 1910), but none is applicable here.

In *Orientalistische Literaturzeitung*, 13: 156–165, 204–210 (1910), Ungnad published a critical review of Gautier in which he corrected many readings. Ungnad also wrote a long commentary on the Dilbat material from VS VII (cited above) entitled "Urkunden aus Dilbat," in *Beiträge zur Assyriologie*, vol. 6 (1909). Unfortunately, he concentrated his attention on the letters rather than the contracts.

Translations of the Dilbat tablets may be found scattered through Wilhelm Kohler and Arthur Ungnad, *Hammurabi's Gesetz* (Leipzig, 1904–1911), mostly in volumes 3 and 4. Summaries of the tablets along with transliterations of witnesses' names were published (along with other contracts) in Ernest Lindl, *Das Priester- und Beamtentum der altbabylonischen Kontrakte* (*Studien zur Geschichte und Kultur des Altertums*, vol. 2, Paderborn, 1913).

Neither the autographs nor the translations of the Dilbat tablets available in these various publications are completely reliable, as occasional comments in this article will show. Finally, three of the contracts (G 30, G 33, and G 41) relating to the affairs of the family discussed here have been omitted because they do not relate to the main story.

and its fields were watered by several other canals and streams.[6] Within Dilbat were at least four temples: one to Urash, the principal local deity, and others dedicated to Shamash, Sîn, and Lagamal. The records do not give a complete picture of Dilbat, but the town did have a pottery and brick "factory," and among those whose occupations are listed in the tablets are farmers, fishermen, herdsmen, gardeners, weavers, masons, metal workers, and a manufacturer of oil as well as priests, scribes, and one soothsayer.

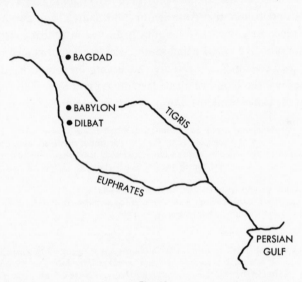

Fig. 10

The eleven contracts in which the name of Idin-Lagamal appears cover a period of perhaps a quarter of a century during the reigns of Sumu-abum and Sumu-la-ilum, the first two kings of the Amorite dynasty. This was an age of expanding agriculture and increasing trade in Babylonia when the construction of new canals fostered the growth of the cultivated area and relatively peaceful conditions promoted an exchange of goods with regions to the north and west.[7] The economic

6. For the topography of Dilbat, see Eckhard Unger, "Topographie der Stadt Dilbat," *Archiv Orientální*, 3: 21 ff. (Praha, 1931), and his article, "Dilbat," in *Reallexikon der Assyriologie*, 2: 218–225 (Berlin, 1935).

7. Many of the date formulae for this age mention the building of canals, as does Hammurabi in his famous code. Archaeological evidence, chiefly the distribution of trade objects, is abundant.

predominance of the temples which had characterized the earlier period was now a thing of the past, just as the increasing use of silver as a medium of exchange was effecting the disintegration of the old barter economy.[8] A brief era of what might be called free enterprise had dawned; or, to put it another way, there had been a secularization of economic activity. As we shall see, Idin-Lagamal and his eldest son, Nâḫilum, were able to take advantage of the general prosperity which spread over Babylonia in the nineteenth century B.C. Their foresight and industry laid the foundations for a family fortune that reached its zenith during the reign of Hammurabi.

Idin-Lagamal first appears as a witness in a transaction involving the sale of a field.[9] Awil-Nannar, one of the five sons of Nûr-ilishu, sold three and a half acres[10] of fertile land by the Araḫtum canal to Marankina, a neighbor of Idin-Lagamal. Called from his own plot nearby to serve as a witness, Idin-Lagamal undoubtedly had no inkling that some day his family would possess the land held by the sons of Nûr-ilishu. Throughout the succeeding decade, we hear no more of Idin-Lagamal, but we may surmise that he worked hard and prospered for, from the second to the fifteenth years of Sumu-la-ilum, he was affluent enough to be extremely active in the purchase of fields and town property.

Thanks to the Babylonian custom of indicating the boundaries of real estate involved in sales and leases, we can reconstruct (with reference to one another) the locations of the fields mentioned in the Dilbat tablets. In the second year of Sumu-la-ilum, for example, Idin-Lagamal purchased two adjoining parcels of land: one in the second month of the year, and the other four months later.[11] His first acquisition was a fraction of an acre from Urash-bâni, a field bounded on one side by the field of Zâzâ and on the other by the field of Idin-Urash.[12] In the second instance, an acre of land was purchased from Lagamal-emûqi, brother of Urash-bâni; this plot lay between the fields of Idin-Urash and Ili-ṣulûli on the one side, and the field of Zâzâ on the other (see Figure 11).

8. Bruno Meissner, "Warenpreise in Babylonien," *Abhandlungen der preussischen Akademie der Wissenschaften* (1936), 1–40.

9. G 1 dated in year 4 of Sumu-abum.

10. "Acres" here refers to the Babylonian *ikû*, equal to about $\frac{9}{10}$ of our acre.

11. U 1 and U 2.

12. The text of U 1 is broken, but the price of 12 shekels paid by Idin-Lagamal for this field strongly suggests that it was smaller than the field in U 2, which was an acre in extent, and for which he paid 30 shekels.

In the eighth year of Sumu-la-ilum, Idin-Lagamal acquired more land: five acres from Warad-Sîn, brother of Awil-Nannar, another son of Nûr-ilishu.[13] This field was bounded by the plot of Awil-Nannar on one side and the field of Nannar-asharid, still another son of Nûr-ilishu, on the other; along its front ran the Araḫtum canal, and to its rear was the Râkibum, a second canal. After an interval of five years, Idin-Lagamal bought the field of Nannar-asharid, too,[14] and when we find Awil-Nannar being allowed by Idin-Lagamal "to cultivate the field of the sons of Nûr-ilishu," we may assume that most, if not all, of the land of this family belonged to Idin-Lagamal (see Figure 12).[15]

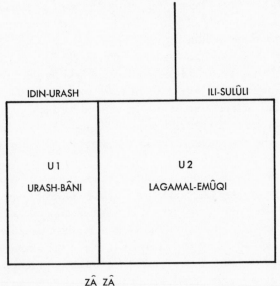

Fig. 11

Still more land was purchased by Idin-Lagamal. Although we have a record of only one field (by the sluices of the Urash canal),[16] the holdings of his sons at a later period[17] show the location of his other acquisitions with relation to the fields enumerated above. Consequently,

13. G 3.
14. G 9.
15. G 6.
16. G 5.
17. See p. 157.

the land possessed by Idin-Lagamal at his death may be estimated to have been in excess of thirty-five acres.[18]

The real-estate operations of Idin-Lagamal within the town itself were conducted upon a much more modest scale. His house, which stood on one side of the marketplace, was probably an inheritance from his father, Ili-amrâni.[19] During the reign of Sumu-la-ilum, Idin-Lagamal twice enlarged his house by small purchases from his neighbors. At the rear, he bought half a *sar* (200 square feet) from Zâzum and

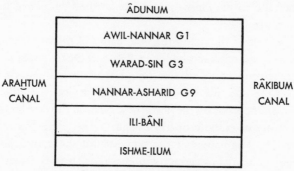

Fig. 12. The Sons of Nûr-ilishu

Ishtar-rabiat, Zâzum's sister.[20] Later, a *sar* and a half bought from Anni-ilum, Idin-Lagamal's next door neighbor, extended the original purchase out to the street.[21] We do not know the size of Idin-Lagamal's house, but on the analogy of private houses elsewhere, his purchases would amount to adding another room or two to his dwelling.[22]

After the death of Idin-Lagamal, his property was divided among his three sons, Nâhilum, Shaga-Nannar, and Tutu-nâṣir. The eldest son, Nâhilum, was a chip off the old block. A score of contracts, dated in the reigns of Zabium, Abil-Sîn, and Sîn-muballit, provide convincing

18. He had bought at least an acre and a half from the sons of Hilum (U 1 and U 2), 10 to 20 acres from the sons of Nûr-ilishu, 18 in the Urash district (when the Urash property was divided among his three sons, each appears to have 6 acres as in G 22), and then he had his own fields inherited from Ili-amrâni. In G 7 Idin-Lagamal seems to be leasing a field to a cultivator, but this is a little early (reign of Sumu-la-ilum) for a contract of this type; leases are much more common in the reign of Zabium. G 8, which is badly broken, is sometimes referred to as a lease, but it could be a loan of seed grain.

19. See footnote 5 above.

20. PSBA dated in year 6 of Sumu-la-ilum.

21. G 4 dated in year 13 of Sumu-la-ilum.

22. A glance at house plans from excavations at Babylon, Ur, and Nuzi will demonstrate this. The average size of rooms is 1 *sar*, while houses vary in size depending on the circumstances of the owner. Some Babylonian houses in the better district might run over 20 *sar*, while the average size of small houses at Nuzi was 4 *sar*.

evidence of his business acumen and even suggest occasionally that his brothers were less talented in this respect.

In contrast to his father, Nâḫilum was active in acquiring town property. Most of his purchases were made around the market square; sometimes he bought houses or parts of houses, but he was also interested in small plots not occupied by buildings.

The reconstruction of Nâḫilum's activities in town is a complicated process, but it is possible to locate most of his purchases with reference to one another and to the marketplace. The method employed here may be described as follows:

As in the case of the fields, the boundaries of town lots and houses are indicated in the contracts by the inclusion of the names of those who hold adjacent property: "a house (or plot) of such and such an area, bounded on the one side by the house of A and on the other by the house of B, on the front by the house of C, and on the rear by the house of D." In many cases the property bought by Nâḫilum fronted on the market square. The names of the witnesses to the contracts are also useful, since the names of certain witnesses reoccur in the sales of tracts or houses which are known to be, or appear to be, adjacent.

A good illustration of the foregoing is provided in the case of two purchases of Idin-Lagamal, (PSBA and G 4) and one of Nâḫilum (G 10). The first, part of a house bounded on one side by the house of Anni-ilum and on the other by the house of Idin-Lagamal, was witnessed by Ibku-ishḫara, son of Buzija. The second, fronting on the market and bounded by the houses of Manniya and Idin-Lagamal, was witnessed by Urra-gâmil, another son of Buzija. In the case of the third purchase, it appears that the property first acquired by Idin-Lagamal (PSBA) was again involved. Briefly, what had happened was that after Idin-Lagamal died, his house was divided between Nâḫilum, Tutu-nâṣir, and possibly Shaga-Nannar. At any rate, Tutu-nâṣir sold his portion at the rear of the house to Ishgum-Urra (a neighbor), and in G 10 we find Nâḫilum buying back from Ishgum-Urra one-half *sar* (the same figure mentioned in PSBA) of the property sold by Tutu-nâṣir. This property was bounded by the house of Anni-ilum on one side and that of Ishgum-Urra on the other, while at the rear were the houses of Ishgum-Urra and Ishme-Sîn. Among the witnesses were Awîl-ilum and Uratiya who both appear in later sales of property in this area.[23]

23. Awîl-ilum is a witness in G 12, and his sons appear in U 3, G 25, and G 31. Uratiya is a witness in G 13, 18, and 20.

During the reign of Abil-Sîn, Nâḫilum bought two houses and several small lots up the street above his house. The location of one of these houses is indisputable (G 15), and the approximate location of the other house and the plots of land acquired is shown in the accompanying sketch (Figure 13).[24] Another house in the same area, purchased early in the reign of Hammurabi, is less easy to locate.[25]

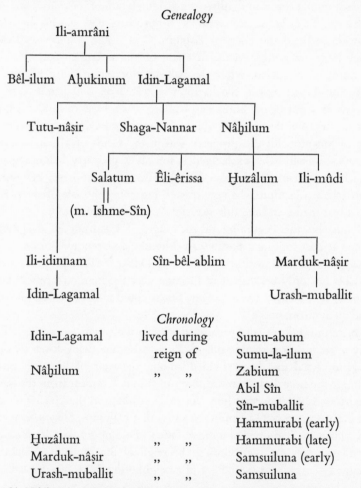

Genealogy

Ili-amrâni

Bêl-ilum   Aḫukinum   Idin-Lagamal

Tutu-nâṣir   Shaga-Nannar   Nâḫilum

Salatum   Êli-êrissa   Ḫuzâlum   Ili-mûdi
||
(m. Ishme-Sîn)

Ili-idinnam   Sîn-bêl-ablim   Marduk-nâṣir

Idin-Lagamal   Urash-muballit

Chronology

	lived during reign of	
Idin-Lagamal		Sumu-abum
		Sumu-la-ilum
Nâḫilum	„ „	Zabium
		Abil Sîn
		Sîn-muballit
		Hammurabi (early)
Ḫuzâlum	„ „	Hammurabi (late)
Marduk-nâṣir	„ „	Samsuiluna (early)
Urash-muballit	„ „	Samsuiluna

24. Nâḫilum became involved in a lawsuit over a house he had bought from Awil-Matim (G 13). From the names of witnesses who appear in both G 12 and G 13, one may conclude that these properties were adjacent, while the fact that the name of Ibkusha appears in G 12, 13, and 15 indicates that the first two properties (G 12 and 13) were located near G 15.   25. G 36.

Down the street, in the opposite direction from the property mentioned above, the various purchases of Nâḫilum are not difficult to follow. This property was all acquired during the reign of Sîn-muballit. From G 20, 25, and 31 it appears that the houses of Namraya and Sîn-idinnam adjoined that of Nâḫilum on the lower side. Then, on the other side of Namraya's house was the property of Ili-zânini which had been divided among Ili-zânini's three sons, Idin-Urash, Ḫunâbum, whose inheritance[26] lay between that of his two brothers, had sold his share to Sîn-nâda early in the reign of Zabium (G 11). The warehouse (U 3) which Nâḫilum bought in the first year of Sîn-muballit stood next to the house of Namrâm, while the half-*sar* plot acquired by Nâḫilum from Sîn-idinam was in the location indicated on the sketch (G 20). Directly in front of the house of Nâḫilum was a kind of boulevard, a narrow strip a little over one-third of a *sar* in area. In the eighteenth year of Sîn-muballit this property was in the hands of a man named Marduk-muballit who exchanged it for other property belonging to Adalallum, son of Awîl-anum (G 25). Three months later, Nâḫilum approached Adalallum, the new owner, regarding the sale of the plot; a deal was made, and the title was transferred to Nâḫilum.[27]

Thus, by the beginning of the reign of Hammurabi, Nâḫilum owned at least four (and possibly five) houses, a warehouse, and several small plots of land within the town of Dilbat.[28] This property was valuable not only because of its location near the marketplace and because of its potential resale profits, but it could also be rented and so yield an annual income.

Nâḫilum did not confine his activities to the town. He was equally busy in acquiring agricultural land. Presumably the fields down by the Araḫtum canal had been divided among the sons of Idin-Lagamal, although we hear nothing more about them, but it is clear from the new purchases of Nâḫilum that Idin-Lagamal's holdings in the Urash district had been large, too. G 19 and G 22 show that Nâḫilum, Shaga-Nannar, and Tutu-nâṣir had divided up their father's holding by the Urash canal (see Figure 14), and then, during the reign of Sîn-muballit, Nâḫilum bought 1½ acres from the holder of a neighboring field, Sîn-mushallim

26. G 11.
27. Because of the poor transcription of the year date of G 31 by Gautier, this contract has been consistently misdated. A comparison of G 31 with G 25 will show that they are both dated in the same year.
28. See the sketch and also the accompanying table.

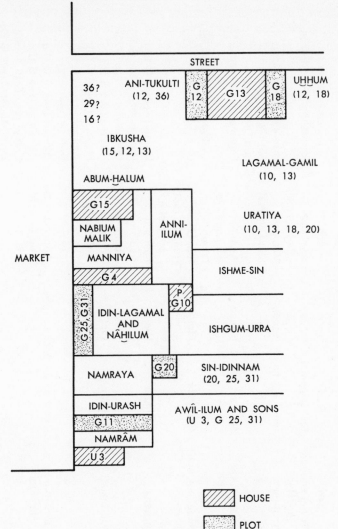

Fig. 13. See Table 1

(G 19); subsequently, Nâḫilum also acquired the field of his brother, Tutu-nâṣir, a large tract of 6⅔ acres (G 22). These contracts are of especial interest because they show that the Urash fields were very close to the property bought by Idin–Lagamal early in the reign of Sumu-la-ilum (U 1 and U 2).[29] This is clear from the fact that Idin–Urash, whose

29. G 5. See p. 151 above. Other fields nearby may be the subject of G 17 and 21.

Table 1.—Town Property Purchased by Idin-Lagamal and Nâḫilum

Contract and Date	Seller	Buyer	Type	Neighbors	Significant Witnesses
PSBA 6 Sumu-la-ilum	Zâzum and Ish-tar-rabiat	Idin-Lagamal	House	Anni-ilum Idin-Lagamal	Ibku-ishḫara, son Buzija
G 4 13 Sumu-la-ilum	Anni-ilum	Idin-Lagamal	House	Manniya Idin-Lagamal	Urra-gâmil, son Buzija Sîn-rîmêni (see G 16) Idin-Urash (see G 11)
G 10 Zabium	Ishgum-Urra	Nâḫilum	House	Anni-ilum Ishgum-Urra Ishme-Sîn Idin-Urash	Lagamal-gâmil (see G 13)
G 11 9 Zabium	Ḫunâbum, son Ili-zânini	Sîn-nâda	Plot	Namrâm, both sons of Ili-zânini	Uratiya (see G 13, 18, 20)
G 15 7 Abil Sîn	Ibkusha	Nâḫilum	House	Manniya Nabium-malik Abum-ḫalum	Ishme-Sîn (see G 10) Nannar-mâgir (see G 18) Warad-martu (see G 29)
G 12 13 Abil Sîn	Ani-tukulti	Nâḫilum	Plot	Nâḫilum Ani-tukulti	Ibkusha (see G 15) Manniya (see G 4, 15) Aḫuwaqar (see G 13) Uḫḫum (see G 18)
G 13 13 Abil Sîn	Lawsuit over house sold by Awil-ma-tim to Nâḫilum			Appears to be adjacent to G 12	Ibkusha (see G 12, 15) Aḫuwaqar (see G 12) Uratiya (see G 10, 18, 20) Lagamal-gâmil (see G 10)

Table 1. (cont.)

Contract and Date	Seller	Buyer	Type	Neighbors	Significant Witnesses
G 16 Abil Sîn	Sîn-gâmil, son Sîn-rîmêni (see G 4)	Nâhilum	Plot	Erishtum	
U 3 1 Sîn-muballit	Abiljatum	Nâhilum	Warehouse	Namrâm, son Ili-zânini	Sîn-râbi, son Awîl-ilum (see G 25, 31)
G 18 2 Sîn-muballit	Children of Uhhum	Nâhilum	Plot		Uratiya (see G 10, 13, 20) Nannar-magir (see G 15)
G 29 Sîn-muballit	Utetum	Nâhilum	Plot	Nâhilum	Son of Warad-martu (see G 15)
G 20 8 Sîn-muballit	Sîn-idinnam	Nâhilum	Plot	Namraya Nâhilum Sîn-idinnam	Uratiya (see G 10, 13, 18)
G 25 18 Sîn-muballit	Adalallum and Marduk-muballit exchange property (Adalallum, son of Awîl-ilum)		Plot	Nâhilum Namraya Anni-ilum	Sîn-idinnam (G 20)
G31 18 Sîn-muballit	Adalallum	Nâhilum	Plot	Nâhilum Namraya Anni-ilum	Sîn-idinnam (G 20, 25)
G 36 3 Hammurabi	Marduk-ennam Urra-gâmil	Nâhilum	Plot	Ippatum ? Nâhilum	Ani-tukulti (G 12) Nabium-malik (G 15)

Note. In Figure 13, based on data from this table, G 16, 29, and 36 are not located precisely, but it will be seen that the position of the houses of the witnesses suggests their approximate position.

field was adjacent to the property sold in U 1 and U 2, appears as a witness in G 5, while Sherit-Urash, a witness in U 2, was the owner of a field adjacent to the one that Nâḫilum bought from Tutu-nâṣir (G 22).

Moreover, Nâḫilum possessed fields in another area: that by the Adad Gate. A badly damaged tablet of the reign of Sîn-muballit men-

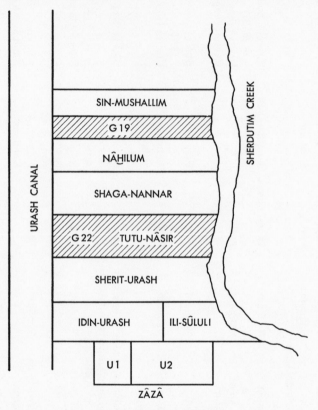

Fig. 14. The Urash Fields

tions a field purchased by Nâḫilum from Ibiq-ishḫara (G 24). The location of this property is clarified by a later tablet (G 39) in which Êli-êrissa, daughter of Nâḫilum, leased to her brother some 10 acres by the Adad Gate "beside the field of Ibiq-ishḫara." In addition, Ili-mûdi, another child of Nâḫilum, is known to have bought land in this same district in the eighteenth year of Sîn-muballit.[30] Finally, there is men-

30. G 23.

tion of a lawsuit brought by Nâḫilum in connection with other property in this area (G 35).[31]

The elevated status which Nâḫilum must have attained in Dilbat, not only as a wealthy holder of town and agricultural property, but also as a responsible citizen is well illustrated by G 32. Awîl-ilum, his neighbor, entrusted the sum of 10 shekels to Nâḫilum—for safekeeping, or possibly for investment. This was in turn loaned at interest by Nâḫilum to his brother, Shaga-Nannar; presumably both Nâḫilum and Awîl-ilum lost nothing by this transaction.

The tablets even reveal a little of the family life of Nâḫilum. One of his daughters, Êli-êrissa, became a Shamash-priestess, and we shall meet her again in the role of an accomplished business woman. The other daughter, Salatum, was married during the reign of Apil-Sîn. In the eighth year of that ruler, a marriage contract (G 14) was drawn up between her father and a next-door neighbor, Ishme-Sîn.

Two of the four known children of Nâḫilum, Ili-mûdi and Salatum, make only brief appearances.[32] Ili-mûdi very likely died young, and we do not know whether Salatum and her husband lived happily ever afterward and were blessed with many children. The other son and daughter of Nâḫilum, however, are very much in evidence. Êli-êrissa had property of her own, presumably inherited since it was located in the Adad Gate and Urash canal districts (G 39). In the twenty-eighth year of Hammurabi she arranged that her brother, Ḫuzâlum, should cultivate nearly 14 acres of her land planting it in sesame and barley.[33] As we shall see later, Eli-êrissa lived on into the reign of Samsuiluna.

The picture which the contracts give of Ḫuzâlum is one of a very substantial citizen indeed. His lease of Êli-êrissa's fields and his rental of an ox (presumably for draft purposes) in the twenty-fifth year of Hammurabi indicate that he was a farmer like most of the other Dilbat people,[34] but he was more successful than some of his neighbors. His annual tribute of 12 gur (about 50 bushels of grain) was large,[35] and he was in a position to loan seed grain to other people.[36] In addition to his wealth in land, Ḫuzâlum had liquid capital and income property. We find him making a cash loan to a lady;[37] and he had property to rent:

31. The Adad district is definitely mentioned, and Ubariya appears as a witness in both G 23 and G 35.
32. G 23 and G 14 respectively.
33. G 39. Three and three-fifths acres in the Urash and 10 in the Adad district.
34. G 45.   35. G 57.   36. G 61 and 64.   37. U 12.

a house[38] and a barn.[39] We can almost see him comfortably established in Dilbat, sitting back and clipping his coupons (Babylonian style), and cutting quite a figure among the simple townsfolk. His prominent position may be indicated by the fact that often when his neighbors borrowed money to pay their harvest hands, Ḫuzâlum was sought as a witness to their loan contracts.[40]

Êli-êrissa and Ḫuzâlum, the principal representatives of the third generation, were obviously prosperous. It was they who enjoyed the real fruits of the industry of Idin-Lagamal and Nâḫilum. The family fortunes were at their peak, and it is noteworthy that these children of Nâḫilum were not straining to increase their holdings as their father and grandfather had done. They were well content with what they had.

A score of contracts dated early in the reign of Samsuiluna enable us to follow the family into the next generation after Ḫuzâlum. Êli-êrissa was still alive. She appeared as a witness to a loan contract in the first year of Samsuiluna,[41] and she continued to rent out her fields and gardens. Her field of nearly 4 acres in the Urash canal district which she had once leased to Ḫuzâlum was not her only property there, for in the sixth year of Samsuiluna we find her leasing an 11-acre "garden" to a man named Tarîbum. In the contract it was specified that 1 acre should be planted in sesame, but the plot also contained date palms.[42] In an undated contract Êli-êrissa borrowed nearly 5 bushels of seed grain, presumably to provide one of her renters with seed for the year.[43] This would imply an intention to plant at least 10 acres in barley.[44]

Sîn-bêl-ablim, one of the sons of Ḫuzâlum, was a substantial landholder who possessed more than 24 acres.[45] He also rented out agricultural implements from time to time,[46] as did his brother, Marduknâṣir.[47] The obvious wealth of Sîn-bêl-ablim points to him as the elder son of Ḫuzâlum, but we are better informed about the activities of Marduk-nâṣir. This second son had land of his own,[48] but it does not

---

38. G 28.   39. G 52.

40. G 59 and 60. Ḫuzâlum also appears in G 43, but the significance of this contract is not clear. This is also true of G 54.

41. CT VI 48b.   42. U 27.   43. CT IV 46e.

44. Bruno Meissner, *Babylonien und Assyrien* (Heidelberg, 1920–25), 1: 195, gives the formula *30 Sila Saatgut auf 1 Ikû*, or $\frac{1}{3}$ bushel of seed grain for 1 acre. Thus, Êli-êrissa may have anticipated planting as much as 15 acres, but 10 is the safer figure.

45. G 48 dated in year 6 of Samsuiluna.

46. G 49 and 50. He also appears as a witness in G 55 and U 21.

47. U 23.   48. U 26 and U 40.

seem to have been enough to support him. Leases running from the third to the eighth years of Samsuiluna disclose that Marduk-nâṣir was tilling other people's fields and also bringing new land under cultivation. He had inherited a portion of his father's holdings near the Gate of Adad,[49] and in the year 3 and year 6 he leased a neighboring field belonging to Samash-magir.[50] In the year 3, however, Marduk-nâṣir borrowed about 8 bushels of seed grain;[51] thus, he intended to cultivate at least 16 acres that year—perhaps his own field and the one he had rented. In the year 4, he leased 3 acres from another neighbor,[52] and then, in the year 5, he leased 3 acres of unimproved land which he undertook to bring into full production in three years.[53] This latter contract is particularly significant because it means that, by the year 7, when Marduk-nâṣir leased a field of 6 acres in the Misrum area,[54] he was responsible for the cultivation of 9 acres not his own. Apparently satisfied with this program, Marduk-nâṣir leased an adjoining field in Misrum in year 8 and also took on a new plot of unimproved land for a 3-year period.[55] Apparently he had discovered a pattern of cultivation which he could follow with profit. His attainment of moderate prosperity is heralded by the fact that he was able to loan seed grain by the year 7,[56] just as his former straitened circumstances are implied by his earlier rental of a house (an indication that he did not have one of his own).[57]

Marduk-nâṣir was not alone in his difficulties over land. By the time of Samsuiluna, the land seems to have become concentrated in the hands of large holders Few sales are recorded in this late period except in the cases of large fields which go to the nobility. Leases, on the other hand, increase in number, and there is a decided effort to bring new land under cultivation. Thus, Marduk-nâṣir was like many other younger sons whose inheritance was insufficient for their support.[58]

The fate of the family of Idin-Lagamal is shrouded in mystery after the fourth generation. Ili-idinnam, son of Tutu-nâṣir, and Ili-idinnam's son, Idin-Lagamal (named after his great-grandfather), were contemporaries of Marduk-nâṣir.[59] Urash-muballit, son of Marduk-nâṣir and great-great-grandson of the first Idin-Lagamal, appears as a witness in three contracts of the reign of Samsuiluna,[60] and then the family disappears.

49. U 26.   50. U 17 and U 26.   51. U 18.   52. U 19.
53. U 22.   54. U 29.   55. U 31 and 32.   56. U 30.   57. U 36.
58. It is my intention to discuss these phases of Babylonian agriculture in a subsequent article.   59. See U 17, 22, 26, 29, 30, and 40.   60. U 31, 32, and 37.

The family founded by Idin-Lagamal is interesting because its story epitomizes the economic history of Babylonia in the Age of Hammurabi. The experience of these four generations was not unique, but one which was shared with their contemporaries. The opportunities for agricultural expansion offered by the early years of the Amorite dynasty were seized by many little farmers, just as their sons were later pinched by the inheritance customs which turned big fields into little ones. The progressive concentration of the land in the hands of a few was virtually inevitable; it is an old story often repeated elsewhere in space and time. We have observed the unfolding of the plot here, and we really do not need the final chapters to guess how it turned out.

Treaties

Better than two-score clay tablets and large clay nails, with identical inscriptions, bear witness to a treaty which Entemena, ensi of Lagash, concluded with the ensi of Erech, Lugalkinishedudu. Dating from about 2500 B.C., this treaty is memorable not only because of the rather lengthy name of the ensi of Erech, but also because it is the earliest such agreement known. The treaty also demonstrates that Entemena and Lugalkinishedudu were contemporaries, something that the various Sumerian king lists do not make clear. Still more interesting is the word for treaty, *nam-shesh* in Sumerian, the literal meaning of which is "brotherhood."

We do not have the terms of this most ancient of treaties, but we do have the texts of Egyptian, Hittite, and Assyrian treaties made in the second and first millennia B.C. These follow a common pattern for the most part. One of the best known treaties, for example, is that concluded between Rameses II of Egypt and the Hittite king, Hattusilis, about 1280 B.C. The Egyptian version, originally inscribed on a silver tablet, is preserved in copies on the walls of the Ramesseum and the temple of Amon at Karnak, while the Hittite version was found on a clay tablet at Boghaz-Koi. The contracting parties in each case agree to establish peace and *brotherhood* forever; they promise not to invade each other's territory and to extradite political refugees; and they enter into a defensive alliance, and so promise mutual aid in the event that an ally is attacked. Hittite and Egyptian gods are called upon as witnesses to the treaty, and the documents end, like the law codes, with blessings upon him who keeps the agreement and curses upon him who does not.

Now, "brotherhood" in these treaties undoubtedly did not have all the connotations of peace and goodwill which the word has today; rather, it implied that this was an agreement between equals. On the other hand, one might make something of the fact that the Greek word for treaty was *symmachia*, suggesting a militant alliance, while the Latin word was *foedus*, suggesting a compact. Nevertheless, with the Greek and Roman treaties elements common to the Oriental ones persist: the defensive alliance, the divine witnesses, and the divine sanctions (blessings and curses).

Although Thucydides gives us the text of a treaty involving Athens, Argos, Mantinea, and Elis, which is essentially the same as that of an inscription which has been found, the classical authors generally preferred to paraphrase documents. Consequently, for the specific terms of treaties we must hope to discover the epigraphical texts which give them. Indeed, many of these have been found along with a great many more not even suggested by the literary sources. We have, for example, the "constitution" of the Second Athenian Confederacy of 377 B.C. as well as many of the individual treaties in the network that allied states with Athens in this period. Typical of such agreements is the treaty between Athens and Corcyra dating from 375 B.C.

This document, inscribed on a stone of Pentelic marble found in Athens in 1876, is headed "Perpetual Alliance of the Corcyraeans and the Athenians" and goes on to say that if anyone attacks the land or people of Corcyra, the Athenians will render to the best of their ability such aid as the people of Corcyra may request; and if anyone makes war by land or sea against the Athenians, the Corcyraeans will help in like manner. Furthermore, the Corcyraeans may not make "war or peace" without the concurrence of the Athenians and all the allies (of the Confederacy) and "everything else shall be done with the concordance of the allies." Then follow the oaths to be taken *1*] by the Corcyraeans and *2*] by the Athenians. The oaths are nearly identical; that sworn by the Corcyraeans reads:

I shall help the Athenians with all my strength as best I can if any one makes war, either by land or sea, against the territory of the

Athenians as the Athenians may request; with regard to war and peace I shall act according to whatever seems best to the Athenians and the concensus of the allies, and all else I shall do in accordance with the decisions of the Athenians and the allies. By Zeus, Apollo, and Demeter, these things I shall do. May there be many good things for me, if I abide by my oath; if not, the opposite.

Inscriptions which provide us with the texts of Roman treaties are not as plentiful as those for Athens or some other Greek states. Polybius and Livy give the terms of a number of early Roman treaties, but it is doubtful that their versions are more than paraphrases. The later Judaeo-Roman treaties quoted by Josephus, who was very meticulous about documents, probably give us something very like the actual texts.

From the last century of the Roman Republic and the beginning of the Principate, however, we do have a few inscriptions which record treaties between Rome and various Greek states. The terms and wording of these documents are fairly uniform. The contracting parties bind themselves to render mutual aid in case of aggression by a third party against either of the signatories, and each promises that he will not allow an enemy to pass through his territory in order to attack the others. In a treaty between Rome and Cnidus (45 B.C.) the two parties vow perpetual alliance, peace, and friendship by land and sea. Virtually the same terms are to be found in a treaty made by Rome and Callatis in 105 B.C. along with the provision that the terms shall be inscribed on bronze tablets and placed in sacred precincts both at Rome and Callatis. In the treaty between Rome and the island state of Astypalaea about the same time we find:

Between the Roman people and the Astypalaean people there shall be peace, friendship, and alliance by land and sea for all time. There shall be no war.

Symmachia is the word used for alliance, because the inscription is in Greek. Both sides pledge themselves to bar passage through their territory if an enemy seeks to strike the other ally. One copy is to be dedicated in the temple of Jupiter Capitolinus at Rome; the other, in the temple of Athena and Asclepius at Astypalaea. Appended to the inscription at Astypalaea is an honorary decree of the assembly of Astypalaea commending Rhodocles, son of Antimachus, the Astypalaean who successfully negotiated the treaty with Rome.

The Legislative Process

The legislative processes of Periclean Athens and late Republican Rome had many features in common. Decrees were prepared by a council, the *boule* at Athens and the Senate at Rome, and then presented to an assembly, the ecclesia (Athens) or the comitia (Rome), for enactment. The assembly would discuss, sometimes amend, and finally reject or pass the measure proposed. At Athens the decree would be called a *psephisma*; at Rome, a *lex*.

This is an oversimplification, of course. A resolution, *gnome*, of the Athenian *boule* did not have the compelling force of a decree, *senatus consultum*, of the Roman Senate. At Rome, a *lex* was a law passed by the *comitia centuriata*, presided over by the consuls; a bill passed by the *comitia tributa* was called a plebiscite, and it would be introduced by the plebeian tribunes who were also the presiding officers of that assembly.

Inscriptions which give us the texts of *leges* and plebiscites are not numerous; *senatus consulta* are more common. But, on the whole, much of our information about Roman laws comes from quotations and paraphrases found in literary sources: Cicero, Frontinus, Appian, Pliny the Elder, Tacitus, Aulus Gellius, and others.

The preambles of *leges*, plebiscites, and *senatus consulta* were formulaic. For a *lex*, the formula was:

X and Y, the consuls, after consulting the senate, proposed this law to the people, and the people duly resolved at such and such a place and on such and such a date . . . the tribe first to vote was . . . and so and so voted first for his tribe. "Is it your will and order?" And then followed the text of the law.

For a plebiscite:

X, Y, Z, the plebeian tribunes, duly proposed to the plebs, and the plebs duly resolved, on such and such a day . . . the tribe first to vote was . . . and so and so cast the first vote . . . Then came the decree.

For a *senatus consultum*:

In the consulship of X and Y, the consul X consulted the senate on such and such a date and at such and such a place. So and so assisted in drafting the decree. The text follows with the notations: "the proposal passed," or "the proposal was not approved."

Roman legislative texts appear in various books of "readings" and in several collections of translations.[3]

As for Greek legislation, the literary materials are not so abundant, and we are almost wholly dependent upon inscriptions. These are numerous, but most are fragmentary and require extensive restoration. The Athenian inscriptions, for example, are highly formulaic not only in their preambles, but also in certain varieties of decrees there are set formulae used in the body of the text (see the following example).

At Athens, until the end of the fifth century B.C., a local alphabet was used for the inscriptions. This differed from the Ionic alphabet in that it lacked the eta, xi, psi, and omega, and the forms of gamma and lambda were non-Ionic: the Attic gamma resembled the Ionic lambda, while the Attic lambda resembled the Roman L. H stood for the aspirate "h" rather than the Ionic eta (long e), while epsilon did double duty for long and short "e," and omicron did the same for long and short "o." Omicron also represented the diphthong "ou." Word division, of course, was not used.

1. ΕΔΟΚϟΕΝ ΤΕΙ ΒΟΙΕΙ ΚΑΙ ΤΟΙ ΔΕΜΟΙ

2. ΕΓΡΥΤΑΝΕΥΕ

3. ΕΛΡΑΜΜΑΤΕΥΕ

4. ΕΓΕϟΤΑΤΕ

5. [ΕΡΧΕ]

6. ΕΙΓΕ

Fig. 15

The formulaic preamble of a fifth-century Athenian decree would contain the following elements for which the Greek text can be seen in Figure 15.

  1] Be it resolved by the council and the assembly (transliterated: edoxen tā bo(u)lā kai tō dāmō)

  2] X was the prytanizing tribe (X eprytaneue)

3. Among the many collections and translations of ancient texts available, the following might be noted:

J. B. Pritchard, *Ancient Near Eastern Texts relating to the Old Testament*, Princeton 1950.

G. W. Botsford and E. G. Sihler, *Hellenic Civilization*, Columbia 1929.

N. Lewis and M. Reinhold, *Roman Civilization*, 2 vols. Columbia 1955 (now available in paperback, Harper Torchbook Series).

A. C. Johnson, *et al.*, *Ancient Roman Statutes*, Austin, Tex. 1961.

3] *Y* was the secretary (*Y* egrammateue)

4] *Z* was the presiding officer of the day (*Z* epestătā)

5] (optional: so and so was archon—erche)

6] so and so moved the resolution (—āpe)

Now, by the fourth century the Athenians had adopted the Ionic alphabet, and decrees often began with a date indicating the year and month. Thus, as in Figure 16, we would find:

¹ᵃ· ΕΓΙ — ΑΡΧΟΝΤΟΣ

²ᵃ· ΕΓΙ — ΓΡΥΤΑΝΕΙΑΣ

3. ΕΔΟΞΕΝΤΗΙΒΟΥΛΗΙ
ΚΑΙΤΩΙΔΗΜΩΙ

Fig. 16

1] In the archonship of X (epi X archontos)

2] In the (number) prytany of tribe Y (epi tās, name of tribe, prytanāās, number)

3] Be it resolved, etc.

4] Y was the prytanizing tribe

5] so and so was secretary

6] so and so was the presiding officer of the day

7] so and so moved the resolution

With all this in mind, let us suppose that we found an epigraphical fragment in Athens such as that shown in Figure 17. We should notice that the Ionic alphabet was used. This would suggest a date of 403 B.C. or later when the Ionic alphabet was in general use in Athens. We should also notice that the letters in each line of the inscription were regularly spaced and that the letters of the successive lines followed the same spacing; that is, that the letters were arranged in columns as well as rows. Therefore, we might assume with some confidence that the number of letters in each line would be the same as that of every other line. Thus, if we can restore one line by using the known formulae, we shall know the size of the original stone and be able to make extensive restorations of the text. Incidentally, it is perfectly clear that what we have to work with here is a piece from the left-hand edge of the stone.

Now, for the restoration:

1] In line 1 we see *epi* followed by what might well be a personal

name, DIOTI . . . If we check the archon list, we discover that in 354 B.C., the archon was Diotimos. Thus, we can restore the balance of his name and follow it with *epi tās*. Then will come the name of the prytanizing tribe (in the genitive) and a number.

2] This is encouraging, because in line 2 we see *tritās* (third), so we can follow this with *prytaneias edoxen tā* (i) *bou*, and, of course, in line 3 the line begins with *lā*(i) *kai tō* (i) *dām-*. We now know that there are 32 letters to a line.

Fig. 17

3] What was the name of the prytanizing tribe? It is clear that it must have nine letters in the nominative, and eleven in the genitive (lines 3 and 1, respectively). The names of the ten Athenian tribes were: Aigeis, Aiantis, Oineis, Leontis, Kekropis, Antiochis, and Erechtheis— all too short to fit; and Hippothontis, too long. This leaves Pandionis and Akamantis, which are just right, and we have to say, unhappily, that it was one or the other.

4] As for the name of the secretary, other inscriptions of this year tell us that it was Procleides, son of Anacharsis, but we do not have the name of his deme.

5] What can be done with the remainder of the inscription is shown in Figure 18. This is an actual inscription (I.G. II², 134), and it appears to be a decree honoring (probably) certain citizens of an unknown city

state. Cratinus (line 6) seems to have proposed that the assembly should
honor these unknowns because they had been eager to do the best they
could for the Athenian people.

Fig. 18

The Cursus Honorum and an Epitaph

Many inscriptions of the Roman imperial period, particularly in the
honorary and dedicatory classes, summarize the careers of men of
senatorial and equestrian rank. Analyses of the corpus of such inscriptions have demonstrated a number of things: the changing character
of the Roman Senate with the introduction of Western provincials as
well as Greeks from the East so that the Senate ceased to be a purely
Italian body; the nature of the equestrian cursus honorum erected beside
the older senatorial one which had originated under the Republic; and
the selection process which tested and identified men of ability from
both senatorial and equestrian classes and eventually determined the use
of these men in the imperial service. The subject is too large for dis-
cussion here, but we can look at a case or two:

Pliny the Younger (late first to early second century A.D.) was a famous letter-writer, an imitator of Cicero who had first made the letter a respectable literary form. Pliny is remembered for his correspondence with the Emperor Trajan: particularly for the letter about the Christians, and for the two letters he wrote to Tacitus describing the eruption of Vesuvius and the destruction of Pompeii.

A public servant and also a philanthropist, Pliny's career and benefactions are summarized in an inscription at Milan. The Latin text with its abbreviations, lacunae, and modern restorations is given below line by line as it appears in the inscription along with an expanded Latin form, and an interlinear translation. The surviving parts of the inscription are printed in capitals; the restorations, in lower case.

1] C . PLINIVS . L . F . OVF . CAECILIVS secundus cos
Gaius Plinius, Luci filius, Oufentina, Caecilius Secundus; consul.
Gaius Plinius Caecilius Secundus, son of Lucius, tribe of Oufentina, consul;

2] AVGVR . LEGAT . PROPR . PROVINCIAE PONti et bithyniae
augur, legatus propraetore provinciae Ponti et Bithyniae
augur; propraetorian legate for the province of Pontus and Bithynia

3] CONSVLARI . POTESTATE . IN . EAM . PROVINCIAM Ex s.c. missus ab
consulari potestate, in eam provinciae ex senatus consulto missus ab
with consular power, sent to that province under a senatorial decree by

4] IMP . CAESAR . NERVA . TRAIANO . AVG . GERMANico dacico p.p.
imperatore Caesare Nerva Traiano Augusto Germanico Dacico, patre patriae;
the Emperor Caesar Nerva Trajan Augustus Germanicus, Dacicus, pater patriae;

5] CVRATOR . ALVEI . TIbERIS . ET . RIPARVM . Et cloacar . urb .
curator alvei Tiberis et riparum et cloacarum urbis
curator of the bed and banks of the Tiber and the sewers of the city;

6] PRAEF . AERARI . SATVRNI . PRAEF . AERARI . MILit. pr.
trib. pl.
praefectus aerari Saturni; praefectus aerari militaris; praetor;
tribunus plebis;
prefect of the aerarium Saturni; prefect of the aerarium militare;
praetor; plebeian tribune;

7] QVAESTOR . IMP . SEVIR . EQVITVM romanorum
quaestor imperatoris; sevir equitum Romanorum;
imperial quaestor; commissioner for the Roman equites;

8] TRIB . MILIT . LEG . iii . GALLICAe xvir stli
tribunus militum legionis tertiae Gallicae; decemvir stli-
military tribune of the third Gallic legion; judicial commissioner;

9] TIB . IVDICAND . THERMas ex iis ... ADIECTIS . IN
tibus iudicandis; thermas ex sestertiis . . . adiectis in
endowed public baths at a cost of . . . sestertii along with

10] ORNATVM . HS . CCC ... et eo apmLIVS . IN . TVTELAm
ornatum sestertium tercentum millibus . . . et eo amplius in tutelam
300,000 sestertii for furnishings, plus interest on

11] HS . CC . T . F . I item in alimenta LIBERTOR . SVORVM .
HOMIN . C
sestertium ducentum millibus, testamentum fieri iussit, item in
alimenta libertorum suorum, hominum centum,
200,000 for upkeep; also for the support of one hundred of his
freedmen, to the municipality he willed

12] HS . XVIII . LXVI . DCLXVI . REIp . legavit quorum
incREMENT . POSTEA . AD . EPVLVM
sestertium decies octies centena et sexaginta sex milia cum sexcentis
sexaginta sex reipublicae legavit, quorum incrementum postea ad
epulum
1, 866, 666 2/3 sestertii, and henceforth to provide an annual dinner

13] pLEB . VRBAN . VOLVIT . PERTINere ... item vivuS . DEDIT .
IN . ALIMENT . PVEROR .
plebis urbanae voluit pertinere; item vivus dedit in alimenta puerorum
for the city commons; also while living for the support of boys

14] ET . PVELLAR . PLEB . VRBAN . HSd item bybliothecam et
IN TVTELAM . BYBLIOTHE
et puellarum plebis urbanae sestertium quingenta millia; item
bybliothecam et in tutelam bybliothe-
and girls of the city commons 500,000 sestertii; and also a library
and for its upkeep

15] CAE . HS . C̄
cae sestertium centum millibus.
100,000 sestertii.

It will be noticed that the career of Pliny is given in reverse order,
with the latest offices—consul and augur—given first. He had begun
with the decemvirate; then performed his military service; then held
various civic and financial posts; it was, of course, as a treasury expert
that he went to Bithynia.

Pliny's was a senatorial career, but a man of his class possessed of
more ability would have held several high military and provincial
commands. As for an equestrian, we might regard the career of Marcus
Petronius Honoratus as typical. An inscription (C.I.L. VI 1625) dedicated
to him by the oil merchants of Baetica in Spain traces his career through
the reigns of Hadrian and Antoninus Pius. The list of posts begins with
the lowest and goes to the highest so that his career is presented in true
chronological order: prefect of a cohort; military tribune with a legion;
prefect of an *ala* (cavalry detachment); procurator of the mint; procurator of the tax on inheritances; procurator of Belgium and the Two
Germanies; procurator *a rationibus* (secretary of the treasury); prefect
of the grain supply; prefect of Egypt (A.D. 147–149); minor pontiff.
This was the normal sequence of offices for an able equestrian in this
period. All that remained to climax a brilliant career was the praetorian
prefecture, but this was blocked by old Gaevius Maximus who had a
stranglehold on one of these posts for two decades; the other, of course,
was reserved for jurists.

As for the common people, there was less to be said about their
lives. To cite one sepulchral inscription (C.I.L. VI 1588):

I, LEMISO, LIE HERE; ONLY DEATH ENDED MY LABORS.

Numismatics

VII

NUMISMATICS, the study of coins and medals, is one of the auxiliary sciences important to historical research. We have already seen the utility of numismatics in the solution of chronological problems, but its applications are much wider than this. Furthermore, it is especially in the reconstruction of Greek and Roman history that coins are most valuable and can be used in the greatest variety of ways.

A coin may be defined as a piece of metal of definite shape and fixed weight, bearing the mark or seal of an issuing authority as a guarantee of its purity and weight, and employed as a circulating medium (money). Coinage seems to have been invented or introduced rather late in antiquity, certainly not before the end of the eighth century B.C. or perhaps even a century after that. Herodotus credited the Lydians with the invention of coinage, and the earliest coins known to us at present do indeed come from that part of western Asia Minor. Although metals had been used as media of exchange long before coins

Two good introductions to numismatics are:
C. Seltman, *Greek Coins*, London 1955.
H. Mattingly, *Roman Coins*, (sec. ed.) London 1960.

were devised, we do not know what first impelled people to adopt the practice of coining money. Some scholars believe that coins were found to be useful for the purposes of taxation or for the payment of troops; others have theorized that the attraction of coinage lay in the profits that accrued to the issuing authority from the seigniorage, or charge for minting. Until the end of the fifth century B.C., however, coins were used mainly in foreign trade as a convenient form of bullion.

Ancient coins were made of various metals and alloys. In Asia Minor gold, silver, and electrum (an alloy of gold and silver) were commonly used for the earliest Lydian and Greek coins. The Persians adopted coinage late in the sixth century, issuing pieces of gold and silver. The mainland and western Greeks ordinarily coined silver, rarely gold. Bronze (an alloy of copper and tin) came into general use in the latter part of the fifth century, and bronze as well as copper coins henceforth constituted the small change for everyday local transactions.

With regard to manufacture, the larger coins were cast in moulds, while the smaller ones were struck from dies. The earliest coins were rather crude—some were hardly more than bean-shaped lumps, but by the middle of the fifth century truly beautiful coins had begun to appear. The Greeks in particular became master diecutters who had no close rivals in the ancient world.

Numismatics, like many other disciplines and sciences, has a vocabulary of its own, and a few of the most common terms should be defined at this point. We speak of the two sides of our coins as "heads" or "tails." The numismatist calls these respectively the *obverse* and the *reverse*. The *type* is the main device displayed on a coin, and the principal type occurs always on the obverse. The type on the obverse of our penny, or one-cent piece, is the bust of Abraham Lincoln, while the type on the reverse is the Lincoln Memorial. The inscription on a coin is called the *legend*: the legend common to all United States coins is UNITED STATES OF AMERICA which appears on the reverse.

On Greek and Roman coins a variety of types were used. For a long time the obverse types were the heads or busts of deities. Each Greek town chose to display its own particular protective deity: Athena at Athens, Artemis at Ephesus, the Sun God at Rhodes, and so on. The reverse type chosen might well be some symbol associated with the deity: the owl of Athena at Athens, the lyre or the tripod in the cases in which Apollo constituted the obverse type, the eagle of Zeus. The reverse often bore a legend giving the city name or an abbreviation of it. From the time of Alexander onwards the portraits of rulers became common obverse types; Julius Caesar and the Roman emperors displayed their portraits on the coins. Beginning with the Hellenistic period there was a great diversification of reverse types among the most common of which were monuments (temples and statues), personifications (Peace, Victory, Justice, Abundance, and so forth), and some purely ornamental devices.

Coins as historical evidence can be considered under two major headings: 1] coins as artifacts, and 2] coins as documents. As artifacts, we might put the coins in the same category and use them in the same way as we would employ the other material remains unearthed by the archaeologist: tools, weapons, pottery, terracottas, sculpture, jewelry, and architectural finds. Coins which could be assigned to known periods might help to date the various strata of a mound. An unknown townsite might be identified by the coins found there; for example, Schliemann was sure that Hissarlik was the site of classical Ilium because the majority of the coins he found were of that town. Like pottery or any of the so-called "trade objects" the foreign coins found on a particular site provide an index to its trade relationships. Athenian coins and pottery occur together on many sites around the Mediterranean, and they tell us that the Athenians traded with these places. Sometimes commercial unions involving two or more states are suggested when the states in question are discovered to have used the same coin types and coin weights. Many of the colonies of Corinth issued coins which displayed the helmeted Athena and the Pegasus which were typical of the pieces from Corinth itself. The weight standards employed by the various states can sometimes be deduced from the coins, and the denominations of the coins themselves can often be identified. Although it is not as easy to establish as some people seem to imagine, the coins occasionally reveal something about economic conditions: prosperity, depression, rising prices, inflation, the changing ratio between gold and silver, etc. Quite apart from their monetary function, the coins may often qualify as objects of art, reflecting changing styles, and related, of course, to the art of gem-cutting. Famous sculptured works or temples and other buildings appear as coin types and may help us to identify unknown sculptures or to reconstruct temples and monuments. On Roman coins we may see the Column of Trajan, the tomb of Hadrian, or an arch or a basilica; the Zeus of Phidias appeared on many a Greek coin, and the people of Cnidus proudly displayed the Aphrodite of Praxiteles as one of their coin types.

As documents, the coins have a variety of uses also. The legends tell us something about language, vocabulary, and grammar, but the legends are valuable for epigraphy as well: the forms of the Greek and Roman letters change through the ages on the coins just as they do on the stone inscriptions; and the Cypriote syllabary and the strange scripts of Spain appear on the coins, too. The coin portraits are priceless. They show us the Roman emperors and their families, Hellenistic kings and queens, the Greek rulers of Bactria and India, and many others. Like the painted Greek vases, the coins abound in scenes from mythology and legend, of religious ritual and ceremony. They can sometimes tell us when and where a certain cult was popular and about its diffusion or decline.

More directly, some coins bear dates in the various systems of chronology we have already discussed: regnal years, the Seleucid era, city and provincial eras, and the like. Very often, especially in the Roman period, a dated coin will refer to or commemorate a specific event. Victories, accessions, birth, marriages, dedications of monuments, and the passing of an emperor can be dated by coins. Frequently, rather important happenings not mentioned at all in the literary sources are known to us only from the coins. It is furthermore not unusual for the numismatist to find a way to pinpoint chronologically a coin which does not bear a precise date. Again, in the Roman imperial period particularly, the coins reveal much about policy, for they were used by the Roman emperors as a medium of propaganda. On the coins an emperor could advertise his achievements in war and peace and drive home the ideas that he wanted to convey to his subjects. This is one reason for the great variety of reverse types which may occur during the reign of a single emperor. Vespasian celebrated the end of the Jewish War with coins which bore the legend JUDAEA CAPTA; Trajan advertised the *alimenta* program begun by his predecessor, Nerva; when Aurelian reunited the severed parts of the Roman Empire his coins referred to him as RESTITUTOR ORBIS.

Probably the best way to illustrate at least a part of what has been said above is to turn to a specific set of examples. The coin photographs and commentary which follow are intended to provide a brief numismatic commentary on the career of Augustus, the first Roman emperor and founder of the Principate.

A Numismatic Biography of Augustus

Gaius Octavius (Octavian), the grand-nephew of Julius Caesar, was born in 63 B.C. Following Caesar's assassination in 44, a reading of the dictator's will disclosed that Caesar had adopted Octavian as his son and heir. This inevitably matched Octavian against Mark Antony, Caesar's principal lieutenant who aspired to rule Rome now that Caesar was dead. By 43, however, Antony and Octavian had found it convenient to join forces, and together with Lepidus they formed the Second Triumvirate. The defeat of Brutus and Cassius at Philippi in 42 and the downfall of Sextus Pompey about five years later removed any reason for the continuance of the triumvirate; Lepidus was pushed aside, and Antony and Octavian became open antagonists once more. Octavian controlled the west, while Antony cast his lot with Cleopatra, the Ptolemaic queen, in the east. When Antony and Cleopatra occupied western Greece with a view to invading Italy, they were defeated at Actium (31 B.C.) by Octavian and his principal commander, Agrippa. After Octavian invaded Egypt, Antony and Cleopatra committed suicide, and the Ptolemaic kingdom was annexed by Rome (30 B.C.).

The victor, Octavian, returned to Rome in 29 B.C. to begin reconstruction and to repair the damage caused by the almost continuous civil war which had begun even before he was born. As the sole surviving strong man in Roman politics, he had very definitely a free hand to make what seemed to be necessary changes in Roman political and economic organization. Although he offered to relinquish his extraordinary powers in 27 B.C., he received instead a virtual mandate from the Senate and the Roman people to continue as their leader. At that time he was given the title of Augustus (the Revered) and proconsular powers with which to govern personally better than half the provinces of the empire. So began the reign of Augustus, as we shall henceforth call him, the first Roman emperor. During the next forty-one years he instituted the reforms that established the Principate, the new form of government that now replaced the Republic. Augustus died at a ripe old age in A.D. 14.

It is not a gross exaggeration to say that our main sources for the reign of Augustus are the biography by Suetonius in the *Lives of the Twelve Caesars*, the *Roman History* of Cassius Dio, the *Res Gestae*, and coins. Coins provide us with portraits of Augustus and his associates; they help us to date many important events of the reign; they commemorate the deeds of Augustus and they suggest to us, as they were intended to suggest to Augustus' subjects, the themes and ideas which he sought to publicize and popularize.

Augustus had not only to reconstitute the Roman economy, but also to reform the currency. He controlled directly the minting of gold and silver and indirectly the bronze, copper, and orichalcum (an alloy of copper and zinc) theoretically issued under senatorial auspices. Of the gold, the *aureus* was the basic coin. It was struck at 42 to the Roman pound, and an aureus was valued at 25 *denarii*. The denarius was the main silver coin minted at 84 to the pound. Thus, the gold–silver ratio was $12\frac{1}{2}$ to 1. Earlier, under the Republic, the denarius had been equated to 10 copper coins, called *asses*. In the time of Augustus, however, 16 of the *as* coins equalled a denarius. The *as* was also minted in multiples and fractions: a large coin, generally of orichalcum, was the *sestertius*, equal to 4 *asses*; then, there was the *dupondius*, equal to 2 *asses*; and the *quadrans*, a small coin of which 4 equalled 1 *as*. The relationship of these denominations is summarized in the following table:

quadrans	1	4	8	16	64	1600
as		1	2	4	16	400
dupondius			1	2	8	200
sestertius				1	4	100
denarius					1	25
aureus						1

Official mints of the Roman government at Rome and elsewhere in the west undertook to provide the bulk of the coins which circulated in that half of the empire; and, as far as gold and silver were concerned, official issues supplied the east as well, but various Greek city states, Roman colonies, and provincial organizations in the eastern half of the empire were allowed to strike their own bronze coins. Nearly 150 such mint authorities are known from the reign of Augustus, while in Egypt a mint was established in Alexandria which issued a special currency intended only for circulation in that province. Occasionally, certain eastern mints were permitted to produce limited issues of silver.

A few of the coins illustrating the life and reign of Augustus may be seen on the accompanying illustrations. In accordance with the manner in which they have been numbered, we may now proceed with a description and commentary for each coin.

1] A silver *cistophorus* (a Greek four-drachma piece equal to three denarii) issued by the commune of Asia in 19 B.C. The head of Augustus appears on the obverse with the legend IMP(erator) IX TR.PO. V signifying that Augustus or his generals had won their ninth victory in the field and that Augustus was holding his fifth grant of the tribunician power. The tribunician power was conferred annually, and, since Augustus first received it in 23 B.C., we can date this issue in 19. On the reverse we see the facade of a hexastyle temple with the inscription ROM. ET AVGVST (Rome and Augustus) on its architrave. This represents a temple dedicated to Rome and the genius of Augustus. This coin was probably struck at Pergamum, but it will be recalled that the *Res Gestae* was inscribed on the wall of a similar temple at Ancyra.

2] The obverse of a silver denarius displaying the laureate head of Julius Caesar. The legend CAESAR DICT. QVART. indicates that Caesar was then dictator for the fourth time (45 B.C.).

3] A denarius with the head of Brutus on the obverse. On the reverse we see two daggers and a "liberty cap" with the legend EID. MAR. (the Ides of March). The coin celebrates, of course, Caesar's assassination on March 15, 44 B.C.

4] The obverse of a gold coin bearing the head of Lepidus. The legend reads M. LEPIDVS.III.VIR.R.P.C. Marcus Lepidus is thus one of the triumvirs for the reconstitution of the republic (*rei publicae constituendae*).

5] The reverse of another gold coin of the same period. The type is the head of Octavia, sister of Octavian, who was married to Antony about 39 B.C. The legend mentions Antony as triumvir and consul designate, and his portrait appears on the obverse of this coin (not shown).

6] The obverse of this silver coin bears the bust of Cleopatra; the reverse, the head of Antony. Cleopatra's title "Queen of Kings" dates this coin to about 34 B.C. when Antony had divorced Octavia, married Cleopatra, and divided the Roman possessions in the east among the children of Cleopatra (Donations of Alexandria).

7] The obverse of a bronze *as* of 23 B.C. showing the head of Agrippa. M. AGRIPPA L.F.COS.III (Marcus Agrippa, son of Lucius, consul for the third time) dates the coin to that year. Agrippa, the friend of Augustus and the greatest commander of the age, was the virtual colleague of the emperor, especially in the period 21–12 B.C. when he was married to Augustus' daughter, Julia. Agrippa died in the latter year.

8] Livia, empress of Augustus and mother of Tiberius and Drusus, is shown on this dupondius of Tiberius.

9] An *as* of Tiberius, son of Livia and ultimately the adopted son and heir of Augustus. Tiberius reigned as sole emperor, A.D. 14–37.

10] A denarius bearing the head of Julia, only child of Augustus. The unfortunate Julia was regarded by her father as the key to the problem of the succession: since Augustus had no son of his own, Julia must provide him with a male heir. She was married first to Marcellus, her cousin, the son of Octavia. After Marcellus died, Julia was wedded to Agrippa. But Agrippa died, and Julia was given to Tiberius. The latter match was eminently unsuccessful—Julia was finally banished for adultery.

The first ten coins have given us the portraits of Augustus and of the majority of his most intimate associates. At the same time, some of the common denominations of coins have been illustrated: for example, no. 4 (aureus); no. 10 (denarius); no. 7 (*as*); no. 8 (dupondius); and no. 1 (cistophorus). Nos. 11 and 12 will illustrate respectively the sestertius and the quadrans.

11] The reverse of a sestertius. The s.c. indicates that the coinage was issued by authority of the senate (*senatus consultum*), and the coin bears the name of one of the three mint officials (*III viri monetales*), Tiberius Sempronius Gracchus.

12] The reverse of a quadrans, bearing the s.c. and the name of the moneyer, Apronius Sisenna. As in the case of no. 11, the title of the moneyer is given as triumvir A(ere) A(rgento) A(uro) F(lando) F(eriundo), member of the board of three for casting and striking bronze, silver, and gold.

13] The reverse of an *as*. Again, the S.C. and the name of the moneyer, C. Plotius Rufus.

14] The reverse of a cistophorus showing a sphinx, presumably in imitation of the signet ring of Augustus. The obverse (not shown) bears the portrait of the ruler.

Turning now to aspects of the reign as illustrated by the coins, we may observe the following:

15] The reverse of an aureus commemorating the victory over Antony and Cleopatra at Actium. This is confirmed by the ACT appearing below the type, Apollo and his lyre. Other issues of denarii identify the deity specifically as Apollo of Actium.

16] The reverse of a denarius displaying a crocodile and the legend AEGYPTO CAPTA. This commemorates the annexation of Egypt in the year following the Battle of Actium.

17] Reverse of a denarius showing Augustus and Agrippa standing on a platform, each with a roll in his hand. It has been presumed that the coin refers to the taking of the census in 28 B.C., but it is undoubtedly the later census of 13 B.C. that is commemorated here because of the known date of the moneyer, C. Marius.

18] Speaking of the events of 27 B.C., Augustus says in the *Res Gestae* (XXXIV): "I was given the title of Augustus by senatorial decree, and by public decree the doorposts of my dwelling were covered with laurel, and a civic crown was fixed over my door, and a golden shield was deposited in the Curia Julia. . . ." On the reverse of this denarius we see the laurel crown and a shield on which is inscribed S.P.Q.R. CL.V (clupeus virtutis), and the coin bears the legend OB CIVES SERVATOS.

19] Augustus narrowly escaped death in Spain when a bolt of lightning killed the man next to him. In gratitude for his escape he dedicated a temple to Jupiter Tonans in Rome in 22 B.C. Here we see the reverse of a denarius displaying a temple within which is a statue of Jupiter. The legend is IOV(is) TON(antis).

20] In Ch. XXIX of the *Res Gestae* we read, "The plunder and standards of three Roman armies I forced the Parthians to return to me." The legend on the reverse of this denarius is SIGNIS PARTHICIS RECEPTIS. This was a great triumph for Augustus because the most important trophies returned were those which Crassus had lost at Carrhae in 53 B.C. The date of this major diplomatic success was 20 B.C.

21] In the same year Augustus significantly dedicated at Rome the temple of Mars the Avenger. The temple appears on the reverse of this denarius with the legend MARTIS VLTORIS.

22] In 19 B.C. when Augustus returned to Rome from the East, the Senate honored him by consecrating an altar to Fortuna Redux. The altar appears on the reverse of this denarius. The inscription reads FORT.RED.CAES.AVG.S.P.Q.R.

23] The Secular Games, for which Horace composed the Carmen Saeculare, were celebrated in 17 B.C. These ceremonies were intended to herald the beginning of a new era, or *saeculum*: this, as Virgil had predicted, was to be a Golden Age. The Secular Games, like the return of the standards by the Parthians, served very well the campaign of Augustus to revive the morale and optimism of the Romans which had been sadly damaged by the civil wars. A *saeculum* was always heralded by signs and portents. A comet had appeared in 43 B.C., and normally the Romans would have begun the new era then, but the times were hardly propitious. When the comet returned in 17, the time was clearly ripe for the change. We see the comet on this denarius along with the legend DIVVS IVLIVS (the deified Julius). Caesar was associated with the comet because it had first appeared shortly after his assassination.

24] Referring to a decision of 16 B.C., the *Res Gestae* says, "The Senate decreed that every fifth year vows should be undertaken for my health by the consuls and priests (vota pro valetudine mea suscipi per consules et sacerdotes quinto quoque anno senatus decrevit)." On the reverse of this denarius within an oak-wreath we see the legend: IOVI VOI. SVSC. PRO. SAL. CAES. AVG. S.P.Q.R. Our coin has *pro salute* instead of *pro valetudine*, but other coin legends are known which follow the wording of the *Res Gestae* more closely.

25] In 12 B.C. after the death of Lepidus, who had been Pontifex Maximus since Caesar's assassination, Augustus was elected to that high religious post. This reverse shows a tablet or stele on which is inscribed C(omitia) C(aesaris) AVGVSTI. This refers to the vote of the assembly which elected Augustus Pontifex Maximus.

26] Augustus had hoped to establish his grandsons, Gaius and Lucius, as his successors. They were launched into public life and office-holding long before the customary age, and their grandfather took great pains to advertise their eligibility. The reverse of this denarius shows Gaius and Lucius, mere boys, at the very beginning of the Christian era. Within four years, both had died.

27] Statues and portrait busts of Augustus were everywhere in Rome. The one we know best is the standing figure of Augustus in military costume with hand upraised. The same statue must be portrayed on this coin.

28] The reverse of a denarius showing an equestrian statue of Augustus.

29] The reverse of an aureus shows a triumphal arch celebrating the Parthian victories.

30] Peace was a theme of Augustan propaganda. The dedication of the Ara Pacis in 13 B.C. was a piece of propaganda similar to the Ludi Saeculares of four years earlier. Pax (peace) also appears on this cistophorus from Asia.

31] Augustus, like Julius Caesar, was deified after his death. On the obverse of this dupondius we see him with a radiate crown and the legend DIVVS AVGVSTVS PATER.

Conclusion

HERE we stop, but let no one imagine that we have exhausted the subject. In this brief and elementary introduction whole categories of source materials and many types of problems have not even been mentioned. Linguistics has been slighted, and innumerable facets of archaeology have been left unexplored.

Enough has been said, however, to suggest some things worth knowing about the ancient field. It should be clear that the sources of information we already possess have not been fully exploited. There is much to be learned from what we now have and from what will be discovered in the future. And, furthermore, while the story of the past will always fascinate us, the inquiring mind will discover excitement and challenge in the variety and difficulty of the problems presented by the fragmentary remains of Near Eastern and classical antiquity.

Index